Confessions
Of A
Special Eddie:

Reflections In Appreciation
Of Human Difference

T. Mark Costello

≈ *Wizard Press* ≈
New York

Confessions Of A
Special Eddie:
Reflections In Appreciation
Of Human Difference

Wizard Press
149-40 7th Avenue
Whitestone, New York 11357

ISBN # 1-881135-04-7

To Ryan, whose essence
radiated the meaning of the human spirit in
such a manner as to inspire others to accept
the challenges of life in larger steps.

Acknowledgments

When one only pauses once in his lifetime to attempt something of a literary nature, it seems more essential that he pay thanks to those whose contributions to this effort have been meaningful. With that in mind, let me express my deepest appreciation to the following people for a wide variety of reasons.

≈ To my late parents for demonstrating so vividly by their example that it is truly greater to give than to receive.

≈ To my wife, Carol, and our children, Tommy, Kevin, and Monica for their support for an understanding of my "other love" and "other kids."

≈ To each and every child who allowed me the opportunity to share in the uniqueness of its childhood.

≈ To my colleagues and friends, those for and with whom I worked, who share in the enthusiasm for life that is a by-product of special education.

≈ To Ramon Rocha, Howie Sanford and Lyle Lehman whose efforts at S.U.C. Geneseo provided me with the highest quality special education teachers to serve our children with such effectiveness.

≈ To Dan Sage at Syracuse University whose selfless commitment to "mentoring" his students has inspired us never to forget that we are all teachers at heart.

≈ To the late Senator Jim Donavan whose tireless legislative efforts provided our profession with the power in New York State to insure that all exceptional children had the opportunity to experience success.

≈ To Fred Weintraub whose counsel and example always replenish our wellspring of enthusiasm for our work with children with disabilities.

≈ To Barbara Skrapits whose encouragement resulted in the motivation to attempt to record for others the wonderment of our work with exceptional individuals.

Preface

*E*ach workday for the past quarter century has given me the opportunity to observe a quiet but determined revolution taking place in our society. As a teacher, administrator, lobbyist, student, and citizen, I have experienced with joy and enthusiasm the process through which our nation became further aware of the needs and rights of those of us we rightfully refer to as exceptional. This sociological, educational, and political metamorphosis occurred, ironically, during an historical period when many Americans were questioning the viability of many of our governmental and cultural institutions.

Early in my career, as a teacher of children with mental retardation, I grew frustrated with those, who when hearing of my work, responded by saying, "You must have a lot of patience." In response to their observation, I carefully countered, "No, as a matter of fact, I have very little patience. But then again, I don't really need to, for you see I'd rather have one hundred percent of fifty than fifty percent of one hundred. While my students may only possess an IQ of fifty, they give me a one hundred percent effort. If I were confronted with children whose IQs were average, and they only gave me a minimal effort, I would need patience or they might become patients."

While the mathematical equation above may result in a similar answer (fifty), the motivational and inspirational factors inherent in its reality have served to excite special educators and child advocates throughout the past three decades. Working with children who respond with diligence and enthusiasm, despite complex and confusing handicapping conditions, to the challenges of being an able learner is a unique privilege I have shared with far too few called educators.

Good fortune has provided me with opportunities to

work with children at all extremes of our social, economic, and educational systems. Wealth and poverty, giftedness and retardation, child abuse and overindulgence, hyperactivity and autism, cosmopolitan and homeless are contrasting characteristics that describe the work world in which I have functioned. Finding joy and satisfaction has been, however, both challenging and easy. Playing an ongoing role on this stage of social revolution while still being involved on a daily basis with delivering services to our children has been both fulfilling and rewarding.

My need to record my many meaningful learning experiences may far exceed your need to read about them. It is, however, my sincere hope that by reading about the children I've taught, the teachers and administrators I've worked with, and the most important political process in the history of public education, you will somehow experience the joy and pride I have in my profession and my country's system of governance.

It is said that human difference, not unlike beauty, is in the eye of the beholder. Believing in the educability of intelligence and the excitement of human potential drive special educators to dream of successes that others consider out of reach. Such optimism and determination inspire many of us to embrace a strong desire for touching others through the written word in a manner consistent with the impact that exceptional children have had on our lives.

The intent of this literary effort is to contribute in a meaningful manner to the recorded history of attitudinal change regarding those who are different. It is hoped, that by introducing the people and experiences involved in this change, the readers's faith in both democracy and human potential will be restored. Few people can say that they have loved every day of their adult work life. Maybe they should have given greater consideration to a career in special education.

The names of students have been changed out of respect for their privacy.

Table of Contents

Introduction

On The Beauty of Human Difference

*M*any years ago a talented author wrote a book titled **Travels with Charlie**, in which he described his trip around the United States with his pet dog. An instant best seller, this tale of fun-filled adventure captivated readers with its honesty and simplicity.

Although my own opportunities to see the world have been rather limited during the first half century of my life, I have enjoyed a less conventional though far more rewarding journey. I have been blessed with a unique trip through the extreme reaches of our human condition. It has been a voyage where opportunities to share quality time with the widest variety of exceptional children have been abundant.

From working with infants and their mothers to designing programs for senior citizens with disabilities, the trip has been most challenging. I have encountered both gifted children whose potential for success has been clouded due to serious emotional problems, as well as students with severe retardation with dependence upon technology for basic life support. I have faced the problems of poor urban and rural children with disabilities whose level of need differed dramatically from those whose family roots sprung from the wealthiest suburbs of our nation.

Throughout the duration of this journey, the opportunities to learn and grow via the educational interchanges between teacher and students have been bountiful. Jonathan, Jay, Lance, George, Scott and thousands of these exceptional children have allowed me access to their uniqueness and a share of the treasure known as childhood. Smiles, tears, pride, pain, and perseverance have marked our joint victories and defeats. Special Olympic track meets have no hurdles - but life does for competitors who fight on a daily basis for the smallest parts of the American Dream.

We (students and teachers) have joined together in the effort to change the attitudes of others toward those who deviate from the norm. Today, public awareness of the needs of exceptional individuals has never been higher. Access to the mainstream of American life has been significantly accomplished in many ways. There still, however, remains much to be done before we sleep.

A storm is mounting on the horizon. So much so, in fact, that my purpose in recording these reflections has been solely to encourage you to enjoin yourself with the others who will ultimately carry on the future battles.

Those who have worked during the past three decades with exceptional children will soon be rewarded with years of restful retirement. But, as we close in on the day when our daily professional efforts cease, many of us are faced with increasing legacy needs. The service system we have so carefully crafted will require the commitment and skills of an entire generation of new young professionals. Selfishly, we want them to be the brightest and most energetic men and women turned out by our nation's educational system. Unfortunately, this may not turn out to be the case.

The challenges faced by special educators in the twenty-first century will make the accomplishments of the past seem trivial. The rapidly changing demographics of the nation as a whole cry out for creative solutions to ever emerging problems. Infants born to addicted mothers, increasing levels of child abuse, and the rise of incidence of mental illness among teenagers are just the tip of a complex iceberg. Schools are increasingly being called upon to solve social and health problems that defy easy resolution. History would indicate that public education rarely, if ever, turns down a challenge. Once accepting a responsibility, however, the system usually turns to special educators to develop the services required to meet the particular need.

Young people wishing to play a meaningful role in tomorrow's social/educational arena can serve as special educators, social workers, psychologists, counselors, speech therapists, administrators, or in any of a number of exciting professional positions. Training programs in each of these fields are eagerly accepting applicants, and in many cases, there are scholarships and favorable student loan options available. Summer jobs and volunteer opportunities give young people a chance to work with exceptional children to assist them in decision making prior to selection of a profession or preferred area of disability. I have told many an aspiring teacher of children with emotional problems, "You are going to either love every minute of it or hate every second of it. There is no in between." This is why I believe that personal experience before entering the field is always critical.

Not only is there a wide variety of fascinating and rewarding careers working with children with disabilities, there are also many different settings in which to hone your skills. Local public schools, center-based schools, residential treatment centers, clinics, hospitals and community-based venues are just some of the instructional environments where special education takes place. Well aware that there are "different courses for different horses," it is nice to have the professional flexibility within the system in order to accommodate both students and staff. If your best contribution to the field would be as a teacher of children with emotional problems in an outdoor education program, you have the opportunity to work in such a setting. Should you desire to serve as a puppeteer in a hospital for young children who are seriously ill, your wish can be fulfilled. As the limits of our creativity expand, there will continue to be a growing number of exciting options available for people participating in the helping professions.

While we will explore the where and how of special education, the most important question still remains; why would someone desire to pursue a career as a special educator?

Having asked this question of numerous job applicants, I am aware of many reasons which only reveal themselves through observing the interactions between teachers and students within classroom settings. Each of us must examine for ourselves whether these factors are motivators for a career choice. You must ask yourself whether your beliefs are consistent with those of individuals who have found success and happiness as special educators.

One way to explore values and determine your potential as a special educator is to reflect upon the following questions:

- Do I firmly believe in the educability of intelligence and feel challenged by the implications thereof?
- Am I easily and legitimately excited by opportunities to assist others in maximizing their human potential?
- Do I live life aggressively, rather than defensively, and enjoy advocating for individuals by changing the attitudes of others?
- Am I thrilled by observing the resiliency of the human spirit as reflected by those whom others have traditionally devalued?
- Do I truly believe in miracles?

If you find yourself answering affirmatively to the majority of these questions, there is a very strong likelihood you would maximize your potential for professional fulfillment and personal happiness serving as a special educator.

The increasing competition of the changing global

economy will no doubt result in our allocating educational resources differently. Gifted and talented students will be vigorously supported and encouraged to excel in order to maintain our international position in the world of business. At the same time, however, we will need child advocates who will, through their work as special educators, demonstrate the cultural values consistent with appropriate support for those who are viewed as less capable. Unless we commit ourselves to drastically lowering the incidence of homelessness, child abuse, drug addiction, teen suicide, and crime in our streets, our chances of successfully competing with foreign cultures will be seriously compromised.

By choosing a career in the helping professions, quality young people like yourself can insure that by waging peace through social concern, our country's value system will be the envy of other nations. Immigrants have come to America over the years for a great variety of reasons but the one most frequently articulated has been "to achieve a better life." If this is to be the case during the twenty-first century, it will require a new generation of agents of social change with a commitment to the long established mission of special education.

Weighing all the pros and cons of a career as a special education teacher, and admitting to a slight bias, the bottom line is simply the fact that few other professions offer a greater opportunity to grow as a human being. Each day is filled with activities that provide satisfaction and joy. Surrounded by the most exciting elements of childhood, the special educator is given the freedom to explore solutions to the most complex of human problems. His or her world contains characters and characteristics both befuddling and beguiling. Every morning as he or she opens the classroom door, there is the anticipation that something unusual and/or beautiful will be experienced during the next six hours.

Rarely does the day end with disappointment.

While few who devote their professional lives to education ever become wealthy, those who work with exceptional children experience a richness that defies economic assessment. Through the process of searching for beauty in the behavior of unique children and believing that C.E.C. stands for Cherish Every Child, the special educator finds ultimate satisfaction in incremental progress toward goals others take for granted. Driven by a strong sense of inquisitiveness, such teachers are strong believers in the axiom, "If it is to be, it is up to me," and their behavior exemplifies the level of determination that has been instrumental in the considerable changes within special education during the past two decades.

From my initial adventures at the House of Providence in Syracuse, NY, I have always believed each individual is a product of his or her experiences and the people with whom they interact during their lifetime. The creation of educational options and residential opportunities for children with disabilities has brought me into regular contact with children and adults who have reinforced that belief. Advocates, whose selfless dedication to others affirms the concept that "it is better to light one little candle than to curse the darkness," have seen our nation totally restructure its value system vis-à-vis how people with disabilities are served. Hopefully, by stretching our collective tolerance for individual difference to include those with severe limitations, we have all become more accepting of those whose variance from perceived normalcy is less pronounced. In so doing, we have become a nation which can better accept the charge of social responsibility for each other that the challenges of the twenty-first century will require.

My purpose in sharing my reflections with you has been to encourage you to consider embarking upon a career path that will provide you with experiences as exciting and satisfying as mine. If you are already involved in such work, I hope you will enjoy the opportunity to reflect upon the significance of your professional endeavors. Observing on a daily basis exceptional children whose self-concept is embellished through the skills exhibited by their teacher is a rare and precious treat. Hopefully, you will share my abiding appreciation for the art form known as special education. Reach out and accept responsibility for taking over the paint brushes and easels that will create the mural that will so vividly depict the art and beauty of human difference during the years ahead. Your potential for impact upon the values of your generation is only as limited as your desire to participate. May the children you experience beautify your life in the same manner and to the same degree that they have for me.

The House That Love Built

*I*n the early 1960s, just as today, one of the bench-marks in the life of young college students was senior year. It was time for the parties to stop and the interviews to start. Parents were eager to see the return on their money and the pressure was on their offspring to make the first "really big" decision relative to their adult life. My approach toward this historic rite of passage was filled with ambivalence.

The first night back on campus was, as tradition would have it, spent renewing ones meaningful friendships at our favorite watering hole. Looking at our meager summer savings, my roommate Tom and I agreed to invest ten percent on a few rounds of beer while investigating potential employment opportunities. While Tom accepted numerous hugs and kisses from co-eds who had missed him during the long hot summer, I worked the bar in search of friends who might be aware of appropriate job prospects. Soon after my seventh sumptuous sip of frosty foam, I spotted a fellow member of the senior class sitting at the end of the bar. I remembered him telling me the year before of his job at a child care institution on the other side of town. Seizing the opportunity, while Tom boogied to the latest Ray Charles hit, I yelled "Hey Frenchie, old man, what's happening?"

"Not much, Mark. Working and studying. How about you?"

"Still fighting off thirst. Tom and I are looking to make some serious bread for the year. Got any leads?"

"Sure do. We need two guys to work at the House. Room and board plus $40 a week. It's a great deal, if you can tolerate screwed up kids. Want me to set up an interview with the head nun?"

"You bet, big fella. We'll be over tomorrow with

bells on. And warn the kids that the party's over. Hey, Tom get the other five bucks out and crank up the jukebox. It looks like we may be able to afford to stay around long enough to graduate!"

The next afternoon, Tom and I drove through downtown Syracuse to the West Side, where we pulled up in front of an imposing brick building in a residential neighborhood. Bouncing up several cement stairs to the front door, I tried to develop an appearance of self-confidence to carry me through the interview.

Having been educated by nuns and Jesuit priests since the age of six, I felt comfortable talking to Sister Engelberta about the expectations and benefits of the vacant position. It sounded like a great opportunity to utilize the skills I had developed during my four summers as a camp counselor. Somehow, I think the clincher was when I put down the Bishop of the Diocese as a reference. My aunt had been his secretary thirty years before in my hometown of Rochester. Who said, "It's not what you know, it's who you know"?

The next day Tom and I moved into our room at the House of Providence and took on our responsibilities as child care workers. We were expected to work each week night from 7:00 p.m. to 9:00 p.m., plus an eight hour shift on Saturday or Sunday. Conducting study halls, leading recreation activities, and getting my group of a dozen ten to fourteen year olds safely into bed each night were the primary challenges I faced. Keeping me from carrying out these duties was high on the agenda of many of my young charges.

While passing final exams was nothing new for a college senior, it paled by comparison to the challenges presented by my group of youngsters during the initial testing that began my first night on the job. As I supervised their homework in a small "library" area, they tried every game imaginable in an attempt to ascertain whether I had both the skill and will to keep them on task. Calling upon emergency reserves of determination and spontaneity, my

17

survival throughout that long hour set the tone that would form the basis for my year long relationship with these troubled children.

As intensely exhausting as their testing grew to be during the first few weeks on the job, it became obvious to those tested that the exam was centered around only one singular question. These abused, neglected, and delinquent boys seethed with an intense desire to know from their new counselor the answer to the query, "Do you really care?" Their young lives had been filled with adults who gave affirmative lip service to that question but whose ongoing behavior gave evidence of the untruthfulness of their reply. These experiences bred skepticism and rightful distrust of those who proposed to offer long overdue nurturing. As the psychological scars of their early childhood experiences impacted on their present behaviors, I learned to respect and admire their courage while seeking subtle methods of redirecting their anger and teaching them pro-social skills.

As the fall progressed, I became more comfortable in my role and really began to enjoy working each evening with "my boys." Study hall had become profitably routine for all of us and, looking for productive diversion during that hour, I discovered a series of books in the library by Dr. Tom Dooley. Reading in great detail about his work in Southeast Asia with refugees of those small war-torn nations provided me with the psychological energy and determination to begin believing I could make a difference in the lives of my guys. His courage under fire and the calm manner with which he accepted his own death through prolonged cancer was certainly an inspiration to all who read of this great human being.

One evening while at the House, I heard a sincere call, "Hey, Mr. Cos, come and see it. I finally finished the puzzle."

Recognizing Evan's voice, I walked into the living room of our "apartment." Each apartment had a large dining room, living room, and barracks-like bedroom (which slept

18

twelve) along with the aforementioned library. While not to be mistaken for the Biltmore, it sure beat what the kids had been calling "home" prior to entry.

Evan was a mildly retarded fourteen year old who was the quiet and always controlled leader of the group. Sister Elsa and I rarely needed to correct his behavior, and we could always rely on his help when the going got tough. Tall, well-built and proud, his athletic skills were the envy of every competitive male living at the House.

As Evan led me over to a card table sitting in the middle of the living room, it was obvious how proud he was of his accomplishment. Eager to lavish him with praise, I looked down at the table to see the three hundred jigsaw pieces carefully connected after many evenings of effort. Pride quickly turned to confusion, however, when it became apparent that the picture was face down on the card table.

"What picture, Mr. Cos?" Evan asked.

"Do you see the picture on the top of the box the pieces came in, my friend?" I asked.

"Sure, what about it?"

"Well, that picture is now upside down on this card table and you, old buddy, have just completed one heck of a tough task."

While the other boys were trying to read Evan's reaction to this perplexing bit of news, I began to internalize my first real lesson about the significance of mental retardation. Naive but determined, he had stuck to a task few if any youths of normal intelligence could tolerate. Was this just a glimpse of his true potential? How hard it was that night to convince Evan of how proud we were of his somewhat tarnished accomplishment.

As a political science major, I always attempted to keep an active awareness of current events and how they might shape our world and my draft status. It was then, with both confidence and trepidation, that we came home from school one October evening to prepare with our kids to watch President John Kennedy address the nation on the topic of the Cuban Missile Crisis. The good nuns, all of whom had crawled to freedom during the Hungarian uprising in 1956, were in a sense of turmoil as they tightly clutched their rosary beads. I had only the deepest respect for their historical perspective on the potential danger of the Russian military reaction to what we expected from President Kennedy. With a deep need for someone to cut the tension, one of my boys came through in grand fashion when he posed the question, "Mr. Cos, what time does the war come on television tonight?"

Throughout the memorable speech by our President, I sat with twelve troubled and confused boys while a small group of sisters listened, prayed, and asked me to help with translation. Following this inspirational address, my coworkers and I sent a telegram to President Kennedy congratulating him and pledging our support "during this, freedom's finest hour," while silently hoping we would all be around when he received it. A week later, as Tom and I arrived at the House one afternoon we saw one of the nuns with an excited group of boys waving to us. In her hand, Sister held an envelope addressed to Mark, Tom and Frenchie, which bore the return address "The White House." Inside was a letter of appreciation from our Commander-in-Chief, and each of us went to sleep that night with a far greater appreciation for the benefits of living in a democracy.

Having benefitted from an education steeped in religious traditions, I nonetheless was naive to the potential emotional impact of living in an environment such as the House. Our chapel became the focal point for many of our activities, and the nuns were clever enough to realize that the necessary behavioral changes they needed to bring about in the children could utilize the help of divine intervention. Keeping my charges attentive and solemn during Friday Benediction and Sunday Mass was always a challenge.

Once a month, however, I had the opportunity to participate in a religious experience in the chapel that had a lasting impact on my appreciation for a democratic society.

On these particular Sundays, a vast majority of the Hungarian refugees who had come to the Syracuse area during the mid to late 1950s would assemble for Mass at our facility. Their posture and devotion throughout the service (many of them holding young children) gave credence to the strength of their belief in a better future for themselves and their country. At the conclusion of the Mass, they all rose as one and sang the Hungarian national anthem with such fervor and magnitude that I frequently wondered if it could be heard in Budapest. I always left the chapel with a feeling of both admiration and gratitude which resulted in making my work seem more meaningful.

From time to time, the nuns would put together a timely religious experience aimed at increasing the children's appreciation for the tenets of their faith. Such an activity was our Spring Living Rosary, which took place in the gymnasium and offered a unique reflection on both our children and our religion.

The event was staged in such a manner that there were five distinct groups of children dressed up and placed to depict the five decades of the rosary. The remaining children and staff circulated in order past these five stages while saying the requisite number of Hail Marys and one Our Father.

Taking part in this devotional experience, I was immediately struck by the paradoxical casting that had taken place. Depicting the Virgin Mary was a teenage girl whose mother was a prostitute and who herself had been known to encourage some of the boys to explore their pubescence. Standing at her side, as St. Joseph, was one of my boys who had recently been accused of stealing a goodly sum of money from his teacher's pocketbook. Completing this holy triad, the Baby Jesus was played by the youngest and most mischievous of the children served by our facility. Praying in front of them, rather than yelling at or being sworn at by them, was a unique transposition. Only in America, with a deep belief in divine intervention, could we have pulled this scene off with a straight face and a dry eye.

As many successful experiences as we gave our youngsters, the damage that had been done to their egos throughout their early lives was difficult to repair. One Friday night, after a productive evening of activities, I thought I might share the significance of our facility's name with the boys before they dozed off. It was my intention to paint a more optimistic picture of their future potential so they might dream of happier days ahead. "Can any of you guys tell me what the word Providence means in our name, the House of Providence?"

Ready to bridge off the correct response with statements of hope and encouragement, I was ill prepared for the only answer that was forthcoming. "It means house for bad boys and that's why we're here."

I did my best to counter the mood set by this response, but once again walked out of the apartment that night with the knowledge that working effectively with children with emotional problems must certainly be the most challenging responsibility on earth.

When working with any group of children in any type of environment, there is always one who stands out above the rest. He usually has the highest need for attention and therefore continually places the ultimate demands on both your patience and level of mental health. Despite your efforts on his behalf, he seems determined to grasp unhappiness from the jaws of success and joy. Such a young man was Jonathan.

Jon was ten years old when he and I met and began our often strained relationship. He was a classic example of what later became known as an "abused child." His mother had tortured him physically and neglected him emotionally, because of her identification of him with his father (her ex-husband). These experiences had developed in Jon a high degree of anger and hatred for women, as well as a distrust of all adults. While my attempts to get close to him were consistently buffeted, I had to admire his courage in fighting

22

for both his mental health and independence.

Jon's most lovable trait was his high level of unpredictability. Whenever you had him in your group, unanticipated consequences very often became reality. One cold winter night I was the recipient of some tickets for a country and western show at a downtown theater. As we boarded the public bus for our journey into the city, I noticed two extremely tough looking young men in their late teens sitting in the rear of the vehicle. Despite the low temperature, they only wore tee shirts with a pack of cigarettes rolled up in one sleeve.

"Hey guys, let's sit up front so we can help the driver," I suggested in an attempt to facilitate a quiet and peaceful trip. While the other six members of my group fell for this ploy, Jon quickly ran to the back of the bus and placed his posterior in the seat next to the two tough guys. Looking straight ahead and hoping to avoid being identified with young Jon, I listened as he made his first attempt to establish a rapport with his new found friends.

"You know, you guys are nothing but no good lousy punks," Jon offered as his introductory remarks. The two toughs looked down at this four foot towhead with rugged features in a stunned and uncertain manner.

"You know how I know that?" asked Jon of his adversaries.

"No, but go ahead and tell us, pipsqueak," they retorted, making their tattoos more visible.

"That short guy with glasses in the front of the bus sitting with those six kids told us that when we got on the bus," Jon stated with a sly grin.

While instances such as that bus trip had great impact on Jon's lovability factor, our terribly unsophisticated efforts at treating his problems came up short. His slow deterioration throughout the late winter led to the ultimate decision to place him in the only alternative available in those days - the men's ward of a nearby state mental hospital. As always, Jon was a step or two ahead of us and made the decision to run away from the House before we could finalize his change in placement.

Three days later, as I looked out the front door of the House, up the steps came Jon held tightly by a state trooper. Entering the hallway, it became readily apparent that these two had not fully enjoyed each other's company. After I acknowledged to the officer my relationship to Jon and our pleasure in having him back, I listened with anticipation as this six foot four inch trooper tried to achieve closure with his young antagonist.

"Tell me Jon, what are you going to do when you grow up?" offered the trooper.

"I'm going to shoot cops," retorted Jon without batting an eye.

"And let me tell you Jon," countered the officer, "You're going to stop a bullet, too."

"That's okay," said Jon, "I'm ready to die."

Jon had little knowledge about the realities of death, but his experience of life had led him to believe it might be worth the gamble. His courage in the face of insurmountable odds was inspirational, yet tragic. The state trooper shook his head and walked out the door. I looked at Jon and realized that the development of service options for children such as he had to become a priority if our society was to improve its quality of life. Two days later, Jon left the House, and I never saw him again.

My nine month stay under the roof of 1654 West Onondaga Street provided me with educational experiences equal to, but more important than, those of my four year college degree. Each child I grew to know and love offered me, in turn, his unique perspective on childhood. Many of them left the House and have led successful lives in the community, despite the devastating negative impact of their initial lack of familial nurturing. The courage and creativity they demonstrated for me, during the time we shared a common home, has always served as a source of both energy and hope during my professional career.

An hour after the conclusion of my college graduation ceremony, I slowly walked down the front steps of the House accompanied by my parents. While they were rightfully proud of having been able to see their only child successfully finish his college education, I looked back at the building inside which the most important lessons of my life had taken place. It was time to confront the adult world, and despite the fact that I had no viable job prospects, I felt confident that having successfully survived the test of being a child care worker would somehow enhance my employability in the job market. As my father's car pulled away from the curb, I had no idea where I was headed. But, I was damn certain I had just left one of the most extraordinary places on earth.

Entering the Public Schools

As graduation day grew nearer, my father's dream of his only child becoming an attorney slowly began to evaporate. My father was the sibling to three educators who together provided over eighty years of service to the children of our state. He reluctantly began to accept my leaning toward a career as a "school marm." Never one to handle his disappointment quietly, he took solace in the fact that my relative job prospects continued to appear bleak throughout the spring.

Two weeks after commencement, I was sleeping late in order to acquire the energy I needed to effectively fight off joblessness. Hearing the telephone ring downstairs stirred visions of my ship about to come in. Responding to my mother's call, I picked up the receiver to hear what would become one of the more important questions of my young life. "How would you like to teach across the street from one of the most prestigious girls' colleges in the entire United States?"

Two days later, I was aboard an early morning train heading downstate for my first job interview in public education. The principal who had so intrigued me with his favorite recruiting question found me little match for his sales pitch. A job working with needy children in an environment surrounded by beautiful, rich, young women, providing me with preferential draft status, looked good against the current competition. I accepted the offer, jumped back on the train, and wondered out loud about the wisdom of my first adult decision.

Walking me down the hallway to my classroom on opening day of school the principal was careful to impress upon me two factors. First, he knew nothing about this type of student, and he looked forward to seeing me again in June so that I might fill him in on how my year had gone. Second, I should consider myself fortunate to be toiling across the hall from a master teacher who would be willing to share her wealth of expertise with me. He quickly pointed to her door as he turned to return to his office for more important responsibilities.

Nervously entering the open door of my new colleague's classroom, I quickly introduced myself and observed that the group of a dozen teenagers seemed hard at work. Concerned that this scene might be difficult to replicate, I looked for some secrets of my middle-aged peers' success. Quickly noting that on the blackboard were written the workbook assignments for each period of the entire school day, I saw how little interpersonal involvement was necessary between the students and their teacher as long as they were willing to stay on-task. What then, pray tell, was the teacher to do for the five hours of each school day? Cautiously working my way over to her desk, I learned with great chagrin and disappointment the answer to my question -the New York Times crossword puzzle. Had I ever made a mistake in choosing a profession! I hated crossword puzzles, and it was probably too late to catch the train back home.

Soon after 9:00 a.m., while I was getting acquainted with my eight young adolescents, a knock at my own classroom door signaled that I was about to learn my next major lesson in how the system worked. The principal beckoned me out into the hallway with a very serious look on his face. Sensing he was about to impart a significant bit of knowledge, I asked "What's up?"

"Do you have a boy named Lance Baker in there?" he asked.

"Sure do, why?" I countered.

"Watch out for him, be careful, and don't let him out of your sight," he cautioned me.

"Might I be so bold as to ask why?" I responded.

"He's a no good little son-of-a-bitch, that's why," came the answer.

"No wonder you're the principal, here. Lance has only attended this school for less than an hour and you have him pegged already. What's your secret?" I pleaded.

"It's simple, son, his brother was here two years ago, and he was a no good little son-of-a-bitch," said the principal with a high level of confidence. For the first time in my life, I appreciated the value of being an only child as I slipped back into my classroom intent on giving Lance the benefit of the doubt.

My class was made up of children whose behavior, learning disabilities and/or mild mental retardation had resulted in them being sent to my classroom. There were no known ground rules in the referral process other than the judgement of the school psychologist who seemed extremely vulnerable to the whims of building principals. While the professionals displayed a high level of naïveté as to how the system worked, my students seemed significantly more knowledgeable in this regard.

"Why do they refer to our class as the B.H. class?" I was asked one day.

"That's just an abbreviation for the term 'Basic Help' which is a way of labeling our classroom," I responded carefully.

"Not so, Coach," countered Lance. "B.H. really stands for Beyond Hope, and we all know it."

Working in a junior high school populated by thirteen hundred seventh, eighth, and ninth graders was a unique experience for someone who spent the previous sixteen years in parochial schools. Adjusting to the mores of the public school, while this crowded building, which was constructed to house eight hundred students, reverberated with Beatlemania, was a challenge for any young educator. As I tried to develop a greater appreciation for the human value of puberty, the significant differences in behavior manifested by the students during that three year age span became strikingly apparent. The seventh graders were well dressed, polite and even appeared eager to improve themselves cognitively.

Those in eighth grade spent a large measure of their time in school testing the rules and the resolve of those charged with enforcing them. By ninth grade, the metamorphosis was completed and we now saw in front of us a long-haired, rebellious, under motivated adolescent with a cigarette behind his ear and no textbooks in sight. It is difficult to express the rising tide of accomplishment that viewing this wave of humanity caused within me each day in the hallways of our school.

The first issue a fledgling teacher must deal with is the need to be accepted and liked by his or her students. To combat this all too-human drive, I found, was crucial to the success of first year teachers. Those unable to suppress this desire soon became victims of the system and unfortunately fell by the wayside. Lack of supervisory support, meager peer concern, and the inherent loneliness of the teaching profession all contributed to feelings of insecurity indigenous to the beginning educator. Fear of failure was foreign to most of us who had experienced nothing but success during the early years of our lives. Disconcerting as it may have been, it became an everyday fact of life.

Grouping students according to ability level in the junior high setting provided consequences that could best be described as unsettling. Students in self-contained, lower functioning groups were quickly able to lower the teacher's, and the system's expectations of them, until they all reached a general level of unproductive comfort. In addition, I noticed dramatic changes in the behavior of young, well-bred, and scholarly new teachers, who, after a year in such a class, were barely distinguishable from their students. It was at this point that I realized that children either live up or down to your expectations and that the value of the learning experience hinges on this critical variable.

It was also most noticeable within the departmentalized segment of the school program, that teachers who worked across ability levels approached their teaching chores with varying levels of preparation and enthusiasm. Heading down the hall on his way to a first period class, Mr. Chips carried a map and teacher made charts, smiled and walked briskly as he readied himself for his highest functioning students. Later the same day, he ambled slowly by my room with an arm full of ditto sheets ready to hand out to the dullards he must survive the next forty-two minutes with. These differing responses to unequal but essential challenges alerted me to the human factor involved in the process of educating our young in a pluralistic society.

The overall pervasive theme of that junior high school and any in which I have spent time since was quite simple - student control. The adults in the building are expected and authorized to maintain order and provide whatever learning experiences might serendipitously result from this lack of chaos. The health and efficacy of the school usually was judged by the public based entirely on their perception of our ability to manipulate student behavior to productive ends. Advocates for the important role of creativity and openness in regard to positive child development during these important years usually learned to keep their opinions to themselves.

Few Americans over the age of thirty-five fail to recall where they were the afternoon of November 22, 1963. As a first year teacher who was enjoying a free period that Friday, contemplating the upcoming weekend, I was one of the first adults in the building to hear the news that shook the world-John F. Kennedy had been shot in Dallas, Texas.

As a product of a staunch Irish-Catholic, Democratic family, the impact of this news upon my psyche was devastatingly immeasurable. My study of political science and subsequent dedication to working with the handicapped were by-products of JFK's charismatic leadership. How could I possibly explain the meaning of this horrifying incident to my students who would be returning shortly to my classroom?

As I stood in the doorway of my classroom, an unknowing student body hurried through the hallways attempting to beat the late bell totally, unprepared for the announcement they were about to hear. Suddenly, a well-built, athletic ninth grader I knew through coaching raced down the hall yelling at the top of his lungs, "Hooray, hooray the President's dead!" I stepped in front of him, grabbed his shirt, and pushed him against a locker. It was the only time in my entire life I had ever struck another human being in anger, and I realized my career as an educator might come to an end.

Following the three days of intense national grief, a stunned faculty and nearly catatonic population of students returned to school to search for reason within the recent reality. Soon after the first period began, I heard the expected knock at the door.

"Mr. Costello, could I talk to you for a minute?" asked my ninth grade acquaintance from Friday last. I looked around for his parent and/or attorney. "I'd just like to thank you for what you did last week. I had it coming, and I learned a lesson I'll never forget. Thanks again." I breathed a sigh of relief, re-entered my classroom and felt much better about the potential of our free society to survive and grow under the most difficult of circumstances.

Coaching seventh and eighth grade basketball after school provided much needed contact with the brighter and more talented segment of our school population. Their eagerness to learn and grow, and my enthusiasm for rewarding their success, formed a mutual bond resulting in many successful experiences for all of us. I soon learned, however, that not all adults shared my appreciation for fair play and its role in the games of childhood.

Lenny, one of my smallest players, was a magnificent athlete and determined competitor. His quickness and heady play were critical to our team's success. This fact became readily apparent one day to the athletic director of our opposition school who had volunteered to officiate our game when the referees supposedly failed to show up. Within three minutes of the opening tap, Lenny was called for committing four fouls, all of which had drawn looks of disbelief, even from the players who had allegedly been the victims of said aggression. As the tears rolled down his cheeks, I spent most of the first half attempting to explain to Lenny why some coaches behave that way. Later on he became a starting safety in the National Football League while playing for two coaches who were elected into the Football Hall of Fame. Today, more than twenty years later, Lenny still remembers that game, but more importantly, the many fine victories we shared together.

It is said, "position is everything in life"; so, I was very quick to notice just where in the school building my classroom was located-right next to the instrumental music room. With difficulty motivating students, it was always helpful to listen to the drummers drumming against the wall or to conduct a spelling lesson to the accompaniment of a tuba player. Such was the plight of special education classes in those days, but we at least had a full size room with windows and fresh air.

The value of those last two luxuries gained in significance with the arrival of one Billy Smith, my first migrant farm worker with origins in the deep south. A fine, tall, young man, his entire name was Billy Lewis Lee Porter Smith, which he explained was the result of his mother taking on the last names of a series of husbands. Coming to school each morning with hay in his hair from sleeping on the floor of the barn, Billy smiled easily, and despite very little formal schooling, made friends quickly. He knew he would be moving again in a few weeks, but hoped he could improve his spelling ability to be adequately prepared to add on his next last name.

One of the unique features of my students was their obsession with the perceived value of being taller than their teacher. This was extremely bothersome for someone who still harbored fantasies about being drafted to play in the National Basketball Association. Despite the fact that they could look down at me, some of the boys were unsure enough of their measurement skills to seek reinforcement of their beliefs. "How tall are you, anyway?" I was frequently asked. Naturally, I looked for the opportunity to turn this question into a meaningful learning experience while frustrating their need to gloat.

"I'm two foot forty-four inches tall. How tall are you?" I responded with truth and certainty. With stunned looks on their faces, they worked to find the answer to their question. As we jointly solved the problem mathematically, we turned one-upmanship into an enjoyable learning activity that let us all save face.

Our building principal continued to demonstrate throughout the school year a wide variety of leadership skills which gained the respect of all who toiled within the building, be they student or staff. One afternoon he concluded a rather lengthy announcement by stating with expectation for compliance, "Anyone who did not hear this announcement, please send a student to the office." Turning away from my pupils to avoid their seeing my reaction, I was not at all surprised to hear the following, "Did you hear that? They call us mentally retarded, and he expects teachers who didn't hear that announcement to send a kid to the office."

Lance, contrary to administrative perception, was one of the more charming and personable students in the seventh grade, regular or special education. Good looking, self confident, and muscular, he had a way of being right in the middle of the action at all times. While this penchant sometimes led him into conflict with authority, his charm and ability to think quickly usually bailed him out of tight spots. We quickly developed an ability to tolerate each other's point of view, and Lance was able to benefit from small and varied doses of education as long as they didn't distract him from his first priority-girls.

One day as I sat at my desk, while classes passed in the hallway, Lance stood in the doorway bestowing his best wishes upon a series of seventh, eighth, and ninth grade girls. Then he called out "Coach, get over here right away."

33

As I approached the door, he grabbed my arm and pointed at a student teacher walking hurriedly to her next class. "Check that out, boss. I think you should try to meet her."

The next day, I heard a knock at my door, only to see this beautiful student teacher asking if she could visit our class. It seemed like Lance had taken the opportunity to introduce himself, describe his teacher, and invite her to observe our class. A year and a half later we were married, and few, if any, of our twenty-five anniversaries have gone by without my thinking of Lance. At least, I can't say the principal didn't warn me.

The most memorable and disconcerting aspect of my first year as a public school teacher was my occasional visits to the Men's Faculty Room. This subterranean enclave was populated by a wide variety of males, mostly in their 30s and 40s. Having been a part of the system for the past ten to twenty years, they were well versed in the vernacular of discontent. Rarely, if ever, was a positive word uttered about students or the value of being an educator. Shattered self-images, frustrations, and bitterness pervaded this room and created an ambience that was threatening to a young teacher. "Is this the way I'll feel about my work when I am their age?"

After two years of viewing the impact of teaching at the junior high on both students and staff, I made two important decisions:

- My new bride and I would move back to my hometown where I would work with elementary-aged children.
- I was either going to get out of education as a career or find a way of changing the system to the degree that I would never end up like the guys in the Men's Faculty Room.

Little did I know the excitement was just beginning.

Children of the '60s

*T*he decade of the 1960s will undoubtedly go down in history as one of the most unpredictable and turbulent time frames on record. Political assassination, racial rioting, anti-war protestation, drug experimentation and rock festivals all fit nicely into President Lyndon Johnson's concept of a Great Society. Those in search of self cluttered our social scene while all over America suburbia grew at a monumental pace. With this growth came a proliferation of new public schools staffed by eager young teachers who were anxious to refine their skills on a new generation of learners.

While the term "children of the '60s" traditionally conjures up memories of protest and rebellion, for me it helps to recollect an amalgam of unique children that the schools of this era identified as different. With this identification came placement into what was then known as special education, delivered by well-meaning (albeit undertrained) teachers. The lessons learned from the experience of attempting to meet the academic and behavioral needs of these wonderful children were instrumental in the personal and professional growth of those fortunate enough to have been their teachers.

A day rarely goes by which does not offer the opportunity to draw upon those learning experiences when the teacher and his or her students share in the exhilaration of growing together. Sharing in the anxiety inherent in this time, we were able to focus our energy on a daily basis upon those activities that could bring to each of us an enhancement of self-concept so necessary for survival. Together we struggled to do it right, to gain acceptance for ourselves as individuals, and to redefine our school's understanding of normalcy. Thankfully, my handicap of color blindness has never inhibited my ability to appreciate the shades of human

35

difference.

These are a few of the colors that have shined through.

Pat, a twelve year old, correctly labeled as mentally retarded, lived in a suburban tract home and attended his neighborhood school until he was properly identified and placed in my special education class. Possessing a severe speech disorder, few, if any, school staff or students could understand what he said. Because he always acted like he knew what he was "talking" about, it was some time before his teacher challenged his learning potential. By then, not only had Pat developed serious speech and language problems, but he had taught his three younger brothers to talk the same way. Early identification and pre-school programs were unheard of at this time. What a price we paid for this missing ingredient!

Pat was the product of a home where there was a marked differentiation in the functional level between his father and his mother. While he demonstrated serious deficiencies in self-help skills that were traditionally the teaching responsibility of his mother (eating, dressing, etc.), he would ramble on at great length about theoretical concepts in fishing that his father had explained to him some time ago. I never could quite understand that cognitive paradox to my own satisfaction.

My ongoing efforts to convince my colleagues of the human potential manifest within my classroom were rewarded that spring when the building principal proudly announced that Pat was going to play a trumpet solo in the school music presentation. Practicing with great diligence, Pat prepared himself with unusual calmness for this high pressure performance. The principal was scared, the music teacher nervous, and I stood full of hope in the wings "just in case." As Pat played each of his two numbers flawlessly, my attention was drawn to the members of the sixth grade band who sat in a group behind the soloist. As he played, they whispered words of encouragement barely audible and hung on every note, a measure of support that transfixed my observation. It suddenly dawned on me that never before had these fortunate, well bred young people had the opportunity to cheer for an underdog in real life. As he successfully completed his musical efforts, they sprang from their seats and applauded his exit. Pat calmly left the stage as if nothing exceptional had occurred, but I had for the first time seen who the real benefactors of mainstreaming are. Those sixth graders learned to appreciate individuality through the vehicle of music. They also learned that through hard work, human dignity can abound in all children regardless of limitation or disability.

Teaching **Ricky**, an eleven year old, culturally deprived child with mental retardation, resulted in my first opportunity to experience the impact of rural poverty on our society. Small and thin, he possessed a most mischievous twinkle in his eye that led me to believe he would survive in the face of adversity. He responded well to a tight classroom structure and demonstrated good learning potential when appropriately prodded.

At this time, teachers were expected to make annual home visits in order to grow in appreciation of how their environment impacted on each individual learner. Pulling up in front of Ricky's residence, I carefully studied the one story stone house which must have been built around the turn of the century for some other purpose. Upon entering, I walked across a dirt floor to a chair his mother pointed to. Once seated, a rabbit ran and jumped onto my lap and a bird flew over and landed on my shoulder. Quite a contrast from my urban and suburban upbringing, I enjoyed having Ricky introduce me to his numerous siblings while his mother gave new significance to the word overwhelmed. Some weeks later, as was my habit, I stood in my classroom doorway to welcome each child as he or she arrived in the morning. As Ricky walked down the hall toward me with his head down, I sensed something was wrong. Hustling by me, he rushed to his seat and began his morning work.

Looking at him from my desk, I could tell by his forlorn appearance that something was drastically wrong, but for the life of me I couldn't put my finger on it. Suddenly he rushed up to my desk and dropped off a note from his mother which read, "He's done it again. He shaved off his eyebrows." I never bothered to ask why, but was even more surprised when he told me he used a straight razor to do the job.

The special education classroom of three decades ago was primarily populated by male students. The few girls placed in these classes were a welcome addition and created a more normalized environment in which to learn and grow. One of the most beautiful children of the '60s was **Ann**, a fourteen year old student who was in special education for much of her school life. Despite being unusually tall, her level of retardation caused those of us who had the pleasure of dealing with her to treat Ann like a first or second grade child. Since she functioned at that level academically, we were easy victims of this type of limited thinking. Our class was located in an elementary school, which only further contributed to that characterization.

That fall we held an Open House Night for the parents in our school. This was an event we all looked forward to. Ann explained to me that she would be attending with her mom, a widow, and her siblings. Early in the evening, I sat at my desk awaiting our first visitor. Upon looking up, I saw standing in the doorway my little Ann next to an attractive young woman who appeared to be in her late teens. Anxious to make the introductions, Ann brought this young lady, along with her mother, over to my desk. As I stood in anticipation, Ann proudly proclaimed, "Mr. Costello, I would like you to meet my twin sister. She's also fourteen and goes to Junior High."

Stunned by this revelation, I hoped for the opportunity to somehow make Ann's twin as proud of her sister as Ann was of her. Only recently have we begun to provide support and services for siblings of children with disabilities.

I sure wish such programs had been available in the 1960s for I would have felt much less helpless than I did that evening. Ann continued to be one of my happiest and most secure students, but never again would I fail to review a student's family history prior to Open House.

The Walt Disney Elementary School was a fascinating and exciting building in which to ply one's trade as an educator. An open school which was attempting to become non-graded, it combined charismatic leadership with a faculty that enjoyed risk taking, resulting in positive learning experiences for children. In such an environment, **Darren**, a twelve year old who combined limited learning potential as measured on an IQ test with the need for tight behavioral controls, flourished. We developed, during our years together, a teacher/student relationship which was unique in its mutual reinforcement. The more he grew academically and behaviorally, the more he motivated me to bring him further, resulting in more success which made him more confident to attack greater learning challenges. The end result of these efforts was Darren becoming what in those days was referred to as "integrated" into the sixth grade on a gradual basis. Ultimately, this forerunner of the concept of mainstreaming led to his total return to regular education.

Throughout my career to that point, I had never received a written evaluation of my performance. Always in need of some kind of feedback concerning my credibility as a special educator, I was pleased one day when Darren turned to me and said, "You know, you're just like that guy on **My Three Sons**." At first, I felt pleased and proud to be compared to Fred MacMurray who played the role of the all-knowing father on that sitcom. But then it dawned on me that Darren might have been referring to Uncle Charlie, the other "guy" on that show who always bungled everything. Maybe I should have just asked the principal to evaluate my work.

Defining handicapping conditions has always been an issue special educators have struggled over with little consensus and even less benefit for children. The results of these struggles often create confusion, distrust, and inequity. Such is the definition of mental retardation. The American Association on Mental Deficiency, in their collective wisdom, defines mental retardation as "significantly subaverage general intellectual functioning, originating during the developmental period (zero-sixteen) and associated with impairment in adaptive behavior." Now this is a definition that holds great potential for providing direction for teachers of children with retarded mental development. Take out your planbook and start preparing for next week's lessons.

I strongly suggest a much better definition of mental retardation is one provided for me by one of our so labelled students in a rural area of New York State. A member of our staff visited the farm residence of **Daniel**, a sixteen year old who enjoyed life immensely. When the two of them wandered out to the hen house to gather eggs, a most unusual scene unfolded.

Daniel reached down, picked up an egg and then attempted to insert it into his ear while opening his mouth widely.

"What are you doing, Daniel?" asked the teacher.

"I'm going to put this egg into my ear and it'll come out my mouth," responded Daniel.

"I don't think so, my friend. What makes you think you can do that?"

"I saw someone do this on TV. It's easy."

Continuing his attempt, Daniel grew more and more frustrated by his lack of success with this endeavor. Finally, he pushed so hard that the egg broke and went down his face onto his jacket. Sadly, teacher and student returned together to the farmhouse.

Now, if we explore this vignette of behavior more closely I think we might find a more meaningful definition of mental retardation. What occurred here can best be considered an act of human innocence. Daniel took for granted something he had seen on television, and acted on

40

faith that it was reality. If we stop and think for a minute about what it is we all love most about children and what we attempt to prolong the most -it's their innocence. Reflecting upon this concept has always proven beneficial when over the years I've tried to further my understanding of the term mental retardation.

I first met **Greg** when he was five years old and about to emerge from a pre-school program to enter public schools for the first time. Severe language problems, partial blindness, and a serious hearing loss had resulted in a level of cognitive untestability that led the school psychologist to believe mental retardation might also be a factor in limiting his learning potential. Nothing could have been further from the truth, but the irony in Greg's development ultimately became the paradox that his greatest strength was also his most potentially handicapping constraint - charisma.

Greg profited immeasurably from an extremely supportive family constellation which provided both nurturance and hope in abundant supplies. Medical intervention and appropriate surgery were timely and effective during his developmental period. However, the key to maximizing his potential was the skill of his teacher and therapists in allowing Greg's charisma to motivate them to maintain realistic but firm expectations of him. They succeeded by not allowing him to utilize that same characteristic to gain their sympathy and thus lower those expectations. Fortunately, the teacher of his class of children with multiple handicaps was highly skilled and never allowed her students to psychologically accept the existence of their disabling condition. Greg frequently gave in easily to the temptation of utilizing his charisma inappropriately, but the resolve shown by his instructors was most effective. He ultimately graduated from high school and proved an inspiration to all who had the pleasure of knowing him.

Children with handicapping conditions often times develop behavior patterns which help them to cope with the psychological impact of their limitations. Often, our focus is on the cognitive impact of the disability while our attention to the affective domain centers around behavior management within the classroom. **Mike**, an eleven year old student categorized in those days as educable mentally retarded, provided me with a deeper understanding of how such children build their defenses to survive in a society that desires perfection in its young.

Mike learned at an early age that because most people he had come in contact with considered him dumb, they tended to say unkind or cruel things to or about him. With this in mind, he developed a unique, albeit, annoying strategy for dealing with this phenomenon. His theory was that if he kept talking no one else would get the opportunity to put him down verbally-thus his well deserved nickname in our class "motormouth." He would constantly mumble to himself and when other children spoke to him he would give the appearance of non-listening in order to provide a haven of safety from suspected verbal abuse.

Over time we were able to assure Mike that our classroom was a safe and accepting environment where respect for each other was a crucial dynamic in our coopera-tive learning relationship. Demonstrating noticeable growth and trust, he still, however, harbored an unusually high level of hatred for one person-Santa Claus. Around Christmas, Mike kept threatening that if the Jolly Old Elf wandered into our classroom Santa would be sorry. The intensity with which he persevered on this topic concerned me. I warned Santa (the school custodian) that maybe he might want to skip our room on his annual rounds at yuletide. Ignoring my advice, however, Santa bounced into my classroom unan-nounced, catching both Mike and myself by surprise. Before I could react, Mike tore from his seat and pulled aggressive-ly on St. Nick's beard. As the custodian winced in pain, it was apparent that his wire rim glasses were attached to his beard causing a deep cut across the bridge of his nose.

In retrospect, Mike was making a statement by his action to which we should have been sensitive. Santa Claus is someone who is a part of the fantasy life of children up to the age of six or seven. As an eleven year old, Mike resented any consideration on our part that he would be so dumb as to fall for such a scam. While it might have seemed a silly and unfortunate incident, he made his statement clearly and both Santa and I have remembered it vividly for more than two decades.

One of the more exciting aspects of being a special educator is the ongoing opportunity to witness the survival instinct manifested by so many children. These are children who daily play out their hands with the deck stacked so strongly against them. Such a child was **Wendy**, a diminutive eleven year old girl whose sister was also a member of our class. A victim of severe poverty and abusive parenting, she utilized a cute smile, combined with cunning and determination, to win a variety of daily battles. Wendy was successful at manipulating both peers and adults in such a manner so as to diffuse their anger and gain their support.

The limits of her creativity were constantly challenged by the limitations of her home environment. Little did I appreciate the skills she possessed until one day I received a call from the building principal from her local school. Since his child was in my class, he was knowledgeable about our program and was seeking my advice. Every day Wendy and her sister waited at his building for the bus that brought them to our school. For almost ten weeks, there had been an unusual phenomenon taking place in his building. It seemed that every day a teacher reported his lunch missing from the faculty room refrigerator at noontime. In his detective work, he discovered that Wendy waited for class to begin at his school. Then she sneaked into the faculty room and selected whichever brown bag appeared most promising. As we discussed the situation, it was obvious that Wendy must be told to stop this behavior. The two of us, knowing her circumstances, admired both her courage and ability to carry out this deception for such a prolonged length of time before being discovered. Ashamed as she was at being confronted with her crime, I was sure Wendy would continue to find imaginative methods for surviving against all odds.

The development of what I refer to as the communication triad - speaking skills, writing skills, and listening skills - is critical to the professional growth of an educator. Too often, as teachers, we tend to ignore the importance of good listening skills in relating to the children we serve. As a result, we become overly focused on the one correct response we seek as the answer to our question, and we ignore alternative solutions that students might pose. In so behaving, we deny ourselves access to a plethora of learning opportunities that spontaneously appear on a regular basis.

Such was the case one day when, in our open environment at Walt Disney, I visited the kindergarten class located next to my class. Having planned ahead with their teacher, I was going to facilitate an old summer camp game where we simulated going on a hike by slapping our legs, clapping our hands, and carefully following the leader's instructions. In my introduction to the activity, I offered the question, "Can any of you children tell me what a hike is?"

Eagerly responding with her hand in the air was a beautiful blond-haired, blue eyed five year old girl.

"Yes dear, tell us. What is a hike?"

"That's when you pass the football between your legs to your daddy," she responded most correctly, but certainly unexpectedly.

Jay, a thirteen year old boy with a significant emotional handicap, was one of those students who always responded from left field when confronted with a question. His brain just seemed to function differently from the rest of the human race, and it was incumbent upon the rest of us to adjust accordingly.

One day in Jay's class, the teacher was discussing calamine lotion and its uses in treating poison ivy.

"I had poison ivy once," said Jay enthusiastically.

"Really, Jay. Where did you have poison ivy?" inquired his teacher.

"Pennsylvania," came Jay's response, surprising everyone but himself.

On another occasion, I was preparing some raffle tickets for a fund raising activity in support of a men's basketball league I was in. Jay was pestering me to give him some of the tickets so he could pass them on to his brothers so they might help in this effort. I didn't feel that I should utilize my students in such a manner and was looking for an excuse to deny his request gracefully.

"Do your brothers like basketball, Jay?" I asked him.

"No, but they drink a lot," he responded.

As I searched for the logical connection between this question and answer, he explained to me that his brothers spent a considerable amount of time in bars. They were frequently involved in purchasing raffle tickets, and selling mine would only be a logical outgrowth of this social lifestyle.

My final interaction with Jay was one that also taxed my listening skills but was well worth the effort. About to be released from our residential treatment facility, he had come to say goodbye and in his unique manner, thank you. In so doing, he provided me with the most poignant description of the influence a special education service can have upon a recipient.

"You know," Jay began, "when I arrived here two years ago, I was right on top of the junk-pile."

Having read his dossier at the time of admission, I was hard pressed to disagree with his perception.

"Do you know where I am today?" he then asked of me.

"No, Jay. Where are you?" I countered.

"I'm way up on a crane," he concluded in typical graphic fashion.

His perception of his success entailed our staff accepting him at a point in time when he was functioning on the scrap heap of society. We subsequently rehabilitated him to the degree that he was now prepared to be lifted back into

45

the mainstream of the real world. If you listened carefully, Jay frequently had something meaningful to communicate.

For the special educator, the thrill of victory can be an exciting and invigorating experience. Such moments, while not overly frequent, inspire educators to continue on enthusiastically to greater heights. A pre-school classroom for three to five year old children with handicapping conditions was the scene of one such memorable event.

Kurt, a four year old Down Syndrome child, was playing contently on the floor of his classroom with a variety of colorful toys. As I observed the energetic group of youngsters, my attention kept returning to Kurt who periodically glanced at a full length mirror on the wall next to him. As he played, he began to gradually move closer and closer to the mirror and a quizzical look appeared on his face. Possessing little if any expressive language, he would have been unable to respond intelligibly had I questioned him, so I just sat and watched. Finally he dropped his toy, walked up to the mirror, stuck out his tongue and touched it against the mirror. Feeling the coldness of the mirror on his tongue, Kurt realized for the first time that the child in the mirror was himself and a broad smile crossed his face as he resumed playing. Seeing children such as he operating on the threshold of learning, where knowledge is experienced for the first time, invigorates the spirit of an educator like nothing else can.

During the 1960s, the Kennedy Foundation proved instrumental in promoting the concept of physical education activities for the mentally retarded throughout the United States. Always looking for the opportunity to make life more meaningful for our students, we ended up hosting the first New York State Special Olympics competition. Totally unprepared to carry out an endeavor of this magnitude, we muddled ahead spiritedly with a high level of naïveté.

It had escaped our anticipation that entered among the five hundred competitors would be children who were so frightened by the starter's gun that they would be unable to run or swim in response to its signal. How were we to deal with a retarded teenager who refused to stay in his dorm room because on its wall was a sticker which implored "Don't Eat Grapes"? With over one hundred competitors in the fifty yard dash, we utilized a stopwatch to declare the winners. We didn't realize how difficult it would be to explain to a child with mental retardation who had beaten all three of his challengers that he had actually come in tenth in his age group.

Two singularly unusual events will always remain with me from that sunny June afternoon. After reviewing the results of the fourteen to sixteen year old girls four hundred yard run, it was determined that we had a tie for first place. With blind enthusiasm, we decided a runoff should be held for the first place medal. To the starting blocks returned the two young teenagers, one black and one white. Both tall and athletic, they tore away from the start and entered the first turn stride for stride. Throughout the first three hundred yards, they were neck and neck with neither demonstrating a perceptible advantage. As they came around the final turn, the crowd cheered wildly, the white girl pulled ahead by less than an inch and the black girl stopped dead in her tracks. Never before, or ever again, have I seen a crowd so totally overcome with undefinable emotion while reaching out to support a competitor in need. While that race ended suddenly, it had a strong impact on those who witnessed it.

The second scene, much happier in its ending, was a result of the Kennedy Foundation utilizing their influence to insure the involvement of notables from the sports world in this gala event. Members of the world champion Boston Celtics basketball team had joined us for the day to conduct a clinic for the athletes. As the day wound down and the competition was finished, two of the Celtics joined with a small group of Olympians on the outdoor basketball court near the stadium.

Don Nelson, who has since become a successful coach in the NBA, was then a power forward for the world

47

champions. Standing six foot six inches, weighing 225 lbs, most of which was muscle, and having blond wavy hair, he surely stood out from the rest of those who were shooting baskets. As one of his teammates looked on, Nelson decided it would be fun to reach up with his hand and close the net hanging from the basket so that the balls would accumulate and not fall back to the youngsters who were waiting for them. Smiling as he stood under the basket, satisfied that his ploy had been effective, Nelson didn't notice a teenager with Down Syndrome who was coming up behind him. Sizing up the situation, this creative Olympian tickled Nelson under the arm causing him to release his grip and resulting in a number of basketballs falling on the world champion's head. Ever since that day, when I read about Don Nelson being one of the brightest coaches, I recall the time I saw him get outsmarted at the Special Olympics.

The decade of the 1960s will surely be remembered as a period when America learned a lot about itself and what it stood for. Many of its young adults went off into armed conflict, never to return. Some of our potentially greatest leaders had their lives taken prematurely. The impact of these events on our society was yet to be seen.

The children for whom I played the role of teacher during that period of time were for the most part oblivious to the social and political unrest around us. Remembrances, therefore, are of happy days filled with the satisfaction of knowing that hard work brought success to children who thrived on being accepted for who they were. In return, they provided magic moments filled with professionally rewarding learning experiences that will live on forever.

A Summer in Purgatory

One of the more inviting aspects of a career in public education is the school calendar. In many cases, teachers are required to work only the equivalent of every other day (180-185 days per year). While many members of the profession consider this a distinct benefit, I found the summer job market frustrating and underproductive. While graduate studies in school administration occupied some of my time, I attempted to broaden my understanding of urban education by seeking employment working with inner city children.

The previous summer, Rochester was the location of one of the first major racial uprisings in the country. A year later, there were still high tensions in the community. This set of circumstances resulted in an excellent learning environment. Working in suburbia during the school year, and submerging myself for eight weeks each summer in the issues of poor urban youth provided me with meaningful insight to draw upon in later years.

As the 1960s concluded, the spring of 1970 led me onto two concurrent professional paths. These paths would direct me toward the center of the activity that was to become the "revolution of righteousness" for exceptional individuals during the 1970s. First, I was accepted and enrolled in a graduate program at Syracuse University in Administration of Special Education. Secondly, I accepted my first administrative position as Director of Education at a residential child-care center in Rochester, New York. It quickly appeared as if my opportunities for professional growth would be bountiful, but hopefully managed in such a manner as to avoid spreading myself too thin and not doing justice to either endeavor.

I had spent seven successful years as a special

educator in suburban schools, and I had acquired a Master's Degree in School Administration. This naively led me to believe I was in possession of acquired knowledge that would take me a long way in providing necessary change agentry as a special education leader. Six weeks during the summer of 1970 was all it took to explode that myth with devastating force and memorable impact. The activities of those thirty days not only changed the lives of the participants, but also resulted in marshalling a level of determination that would change forever how our society would deal with those who are different.

At the suggestion of my graduate advisor, I enrolled in an experience titled, "Workshop in Human Abuse," with total lack of awareness concerning its content or instructional methodology. After all, I thought, the price was right (paid for by a government grant) and what could there possibly be about the field of special education that could have escaped my powers of cognition?

My first hint that these six weeks were going to be unique was the result of my search for one of the books that was required reading prior to the start of the workshop. My mother, who at the time was seventy-two years old, volunteered to inquire at the public library about the existence of a book with the colorful title of **Christmas in Purgatory**. It was evident that she was proud to have found this book as she arrived home, but there was a most quizzical look upon her face as she inquired, "What is this workshop going to be about, anyway?"

"I have absolutely no idea," I responded.

"Maybe, you had better take a close look at the contents of this book before you pack your bags for the summer," she counseled with that air of certitude that so often punctuated her comments.

Slowly opening this unusually shaped publication, I was stunned to discover a series of photographs of pathetic looking individuals in various stages of nakedness. Confusion racked my brain as I attempted to reconcile the visual impact of this human misery with the fact that the author of this pictorial essay was to be the instructor with whom I would be spending six weeks that summer. My initial trepidation gradually gave way to inquisitiveness as I searched for reasons for the need to embark upon an educational endeavor of this nature. Too soon, along with twenty-four fortunate colleagues, I would discover a dark side of our society that had been for generations systematically hidden from our level of awareness.

During the 1960s, Dr. Burton Blatt with a small group of fellow professors and providers of services for the mentally retarded, developed an insatiable determination to eradicate conditions existent within the "back wards" of state institutions for the mentally retarded and the mentally ill. Though initially politically naïve and lacking a meaningful powerbase from which to operate, Blatt and his colleagues recognized the need to heighten awareness of the horrors taking place in these settings under the guise of care and treatment. With this as their objective, the concept of a pictorial depiction of reality as they knew it became a logical outcome.

Utilizing a hidden camera in the hands of a professional photographer, and taking advantage of their status within the professional community as experts in mental retardation, Blatt began to document irrefutable evidence of man's inhumanity to man. This stunning array of photographic testimony, combined with eloquent prose articulating the hope for dramatic alteration of this human condition, became the essence of **Christmas in Purgatory** (1966). Copies of this testament were sent to every member of Federal and State legislative bodies whose lack of awareness had resulted in the conditions so vividly depicted in this journal of public disgrace. The first round had been expended in the de-institutional theater of the revolution of righteousness.

With the support of the Kennedy Foundation, Blatt quickly became identified as the leading national advocate for the institutionalized masses. Copies of **Christmas in Purgatory** soon found their way onto the shelves of libraries and into the homes of those with an interest in our society's treatment of the mentally retarded and the mentally ill. Dr. Blatt's career gathered momentum and he was appointed Chairman of the Department of Special Education and Rehabilitation at Syracuse University, one of the premier programs of its kind in the nation.

It was there, during the summer of 1970, that twenty-five unsuspecting graduate-level professionals would take part in a carefully orchestrated collaborative learning experience. This experience would forever shape many of their lives and play a crucial role in the reformulation of public policy. Congregating from throughout the northeast, these young and middle-aged educators shared an interest in disabled individuals but little else in common. For the most part, few if any of them were aware of Dr. Blatt's work or the intention of this particular workshop. Farthest from their minds was the potential of one man being able to so significantly impact on a group such as this, during such a short period of time. Underestimating the charismatic impression of Dr. Blatt upon his students paralleled, with strange irony, the manner in which our society, at that time, ignored the human potential of those they saw fit to institutionalize.

The workshop itself was structured in such a way as to draw upon each participant's interest in and experience with the disabled, their pre-reading of **Christmas in Purgatory**, and the potential of the group to cognitively and emotionally coalesce around the issue of human abuse. The vast majority of the group were special education teachers by trade, but reflective of a wide variety of backgrounds, both personally and professionally. However, none of this could prepare us for the environs that we were to inhabit during that six week period.

From the very moment he introduced himself to the class, it was apparent that Dr. Blatt was a mover and a shaker, an impact player of the highest regard. His explicit objective was to arouse the indignation of the participants to the level of abhorrence necessary to ignite the need for immediate rectification. His charm, self-assuredness, and eagerness to participate in risk taking quickly endeared him to all of us, and added a requisite quality of excitement to our learning endeavors. After the first two days in his presence, the realization engulfed many of us that our vigorous and indefatigable new mentor would not rest until we shared his sense of mission regarding the need to overhaul our public policy regarding those we perceive as different.

Having left my wife and three young children at our split-level suburban environment, adjusting to life in the workshop took on added complexity of an unanticipated nature. Assigned to a dormitory on campus for these six weeks, I discovered that, with the exception of myself, each resident of the building was a legally blind, soon-to-be college freshman. Syracuse University hosted a summer program each year for visually impaired students to prepare them for entrance into college. Believe me, there was little learning that they missed as they developed mobility skills, note taking competency, and the ability to access facilities and technology. Returning cautiously each night to my room, I also observed that their partying skills progressed nicely throughout the summer, commensurate with their non-handicapped peers. This opportunity to develop a greater sensitivity to the impact of visual impairment was a welcome addendum to the preordained instructional menu.

The initial two weeks of the workshop combined a variety of learning methodologies around the central theme of how our society, within the limits of public acceptance, physically and psychologically abuses those human beings who have been historically devalued. For the most part, the victims of these crimes had been those who reside in state operated facilities for the mentally retarded or the mentally ill. Lectures by Blatt, films, slide presentations, and guest speakers enveloped our consciousness in evidential depiction

53

of the horrors of institutional reality. Analogies between these conditions and the Holocaust were frequently drawn by those who shared their experiences with us. It became readily apparent that those who had spent time dealing on a first hand basis with this issue shared a common bond that fueled them with infinite amounts of missionary zeal for the yet to be declared crusade.

During this didactic assault, the participant's ingestion of large dosages of de-humanization took on nearly Kafkaesque proportions. Toward the end of this two week siege, each of us began to carefully prepare ourselves psychologically for the upcoming reality testing that was about to take place in the twilight zone of the "back wards" of state institutions. Not unlike those who served our nation in uniform, we received our assignments with a mixture of anticipation and hesitancy, resulting from the hope that what we had heard would not be reality, but trustful that those who had testified were paragons of integrity. At last, during week three, all remaining vestiges of ambivalence were to disappear.

Heat and humidity hung on the horizon as I drove the fifty miles from my home to the "State School" in a small town on Monday morning. My mind filled with anxiety and trepidation as I reflected upon the many precautionary messages we had been provided with during our preparation for this visit. We were to stay at the facility for three consecutive days, and record in our participant observation notes our impressions of the quality of life being experienced by those in the care of the state. While on the surface it appeared to be a reasonable enough task, there remained a significant amount of uncertainty commensurate with entering upon foreign soil. Turning into the entrance to the campus, I reassured myself with the knowledge that I would at least be sharing this experience with five other colleagues who were facing the same challenge.

Once congregated, and with introductions accomplished, we set out with our tour guide to become familiar with the numerous buildings stretching across the 150 acre campus, and more importantly, to meet those being served by this enormous facility. Likely by design, our trip began in the building that housed the infants and pediatric care clients, where we were first introduced to the concept of "warehousing" as it related to human beings. Here, before our eyes, were over one hundred babies, whose ages were impossible to guess, lying either in old metal cribs or simply on bare mattresses spread out on the floor. At that point in our history, obstetricians, upon the birth of a deformed or retarded child, were prone to encourage parents to consider immediate placement of such an offspring in the state school, so they might not become a burden on the family. Barely attended to, other than for occasional diaper changing, lay the victims of this decision-making process. Our guide also pointed out to us that some of those in residence on this ward were the progeny of some of the adult clients within the institution, who apparently weren't being supervised as closely as they should have been.

Moving on from building to building, it became readily apparent that this mass of more than eight hundred retardates were grouped for living purposes based on age, gender, and developmental level. Our tour followed basically a similar theme which took us through buildings housing progressively older individuals with moderate retardation and which eventually arrived at the geriatric unit. Only upon completion of this phase of our sojourn did we then venture upon the appropriately infamous "back wards."

Throughout our nation's history, up until 1970 at least, these notorious venues of human suffering had gone relatively unnoticed by our society at large. Six graduate students were about to shed our mantel of naïveté as we entered the next building on a pre-designed journey through human misery. Upon entering the doorway into what was referred to as the "day room," the level of consciousness was unceremoniously overwhelmed by a multi-sensory bombardment of stimuli. Visually, we were confronted with the sight of more than one hundred, semi-naked, severely retarded males, in a variety of positions, strewn throughout this barren environment, with looks of wretchedness and despair upon their faces. Auditorially, we were overwhelmed by the intense level of moaning and groaning that constantly emanated from these language-deprived souls. Out of necessity, we reacted to fight off the nausea brought on by the smell of urine and excrement that had, for years, been adhering to the floor that we struggled to remain standing on. We had just arrived in Purgatory.

Walking about the day room, each of us was aware that our observations were supposed to be keen, but we experienced great difficulty when we attempted to withdraw from seeing what we were seeing. With our shoes sticking to the floor as we moved hesitatingly along, the aversion of the scene surrounding us magnified in intensity. Disbelief, outrage, pathos, and hopelessness overwhelmed our sensitivities as we psychologically screamed for removal from this battleground of emotions.

I noticed that in the very middle of this room was a singular bed which we were slowly approaching, albeit with apprehension. Lying in a semi-upright position was a man with mental retardation who was a victim of hydrocephalus, or water on the brain. His head was described by the chaplain of the facility in one of his books, as being "the size of a bushel basket." As a result, he was totally immobilized and only able to move his eyes, which he did as he observed us nearing his presence with trepidation. At the very point at which we entered his life space, his mouth suddenly opened and he addressed our stunned group.

"Hi, my name is George. I am the world's largest and oldest living hydrocephalic. What's your name?"

Astonished to the point of numbness, we stood transfixed while hopelessly attempting to communicate with this most unique and courageous member of the human race. As we finally walked away from his bedside, it dawned on me, that while George had never set foot out of this institution, and we were graduate level professionals, he was ready and able to deal with us, but in no way were we able to respond to the same challenge in return.

In an attempt to repair some of the psychological damage incurred during our initial visit to a back ward, our tour guide next introduced us to one of the more progressive programs operating within the institution. Located on a ward of adult males with moderate retardation, the program was based on the concept of behavior modification and provided a unique reward system worth mentioning. Each client was given the opportunity, as a result of appropriate behavior on the ward, to earn various amounts of smoking tobacco which was rationed out each week and kept in small cans. Consequently, as we entered upon this unit, we encountered nearly fifty men, all of whom were proudly smoking their pipes on this hot July morning. Had I not known better, it could have easily been mistaken for the faculty room of a major university.

Concluding both our tour and the first day of our visit, we were then assigned to individual wards upon which we would spend the next two days in more in-depth observation. My assignment was to a back ward of difficult-to-manage, adult, female clients in their 20s and 30s. This, I was told, was one of the toughest places in which to work in the entire institution, and it soon became obvious how creative these care givers became when challenged.

The building itself was primarily made up of a large day room with benches and a few chairs, and a series of small cell-like rooms where certain individuals could be kept. Over one hundred women stood, sat, or lay on the floor of this day room while four "attendants" stood by, observing the scene. A small group of women sat in front of a television set suspended from the ceiling. The set hadn't worked for many weeks but for these young women there wasn't any alternative but to hope that somehow it might come on again. Throughout the day there was no attempt made to carry out any activities with this population, and as

57

far as I could ascertain, the role of the staff was to prevent injury or aggression from taking place.

In order to maintain an acceptable level of peace and quiet in the day room, judicious utilization was made of the individual rooms with locked doors and small windows. Here were housed those individuals whose inappropriate behavior had resulted in the need for special program precautions. In one room, I visited a young woman who, during my two days on this ward, was confined to a state of immobilization, courtesy of a device known as a restraining sheet. This sheet had eyelets along the side which allowed its victim to be sewn up in bed so that only her head and toes were visible to an observer. No indication was given as to how many consecutive days one might expect to be the recipient of such treatment.

In other rooms, were women who were either asleep or unconscious for the duration of my visit. Finding this somewhat odd, I inquired as to why this might be so and was told that these clients were being treated with a new form of "drug therapy." It was difficult to detect whether the somnific nature of this medication was to benefit the retardates or the staff who no longer had to concern themselves with their clients' behavior.

Throughout the two days, we were occasionally given the opportunity to visit other back wards for a glimpse of the quality of care in other locations. First hand viewing of such activities as "hosing off" and "feeding time" were essential elements of any visitation to a state institution of that era. A large percentage of the clientele housed on back wards was lacking in requisite toileting skills, and in some cases were prone to smearing. As a result each back ward had a hosing room where these individuals would be herded and unceremoniously sprayed until relatively clean. No attempts were in place to toilet train any of the members of this group.

Not unexpectedly, little or no effort was put forth to teach the residents how to feed themselves, so that when feeding time came around visages of inhumanity abounded once again. The food, unidentifiable as a result of the pureed manner of preparation, was shoveled into the vicinity of the clients mouth in hope that some of it might be ingested. With few staff and many mouths to feed this hit or miss process bespoke the overall devaluation of the institution's residents. Each client was fortunate if he or she received one minute of staff time per meal.

For the most part, those who worked as attendants on these back wards demonstrated little positive enthusiasm for their work. One afternoon, in search of a particular resident, I ventured onto a ward housing young men with severe retardation and physical aggression. In response to my inquiry, a surly, middle-aged, female attendant pointed out a young man hovering in a corner, whose countenance cried out with anger and anguish.

"That's the son-of-a-bitch, right over there," she gestured, with a high degree of venom.

"He's injured me on the job a couple of times, but I've gotten him back good. He doesn't mess with me anymore. Why are you interested in him?" she asked.

"He's my second cousin, and I had never met him," I replied. "I promised his mom and dad I would stop by and make sure he was being well cared for" I explained as I walked away, with a more personally significant realization of why the necessity for change was so overwhelming.

Back on my ward of young adult women, near the conclusion of our three day visit, I made the acquaintance of a nurse who supervised the 4:00 p.m. to midnight shift. Her strong negative feelings about those whose care she had been charged with providing were so apparent that when she entered the day room each afternoon, the residents began to gather together, and the intensity level of their moaning increased perceptibly. Despite the severe limitations of their minimally measurable intelligence, they were able to convey to me how they felt about the nurse. I learned from viewing this scene how much we wear our attitudes on our sleeves, and never to underestimate the ability of someone to read body language or affect in our behavior toward them.

"I just don't know what's wrong with these women. Every day at this time they get restless and irritable. They must be hungry or maybe the heat is getting to them," she muttered as we walked through the day room.

Outside, in a long hallway, we stumbled upon a small group of residents with severe retardation standing and sitting in what appeared to be a line.

"What are they doing?" I inquired of my nurse friend.

"Oh, they're waiting to go to confession," she replied caustically.

"That's interesting. I'd really like to talk to the chaplain and see if he feels these people are capable of committing mortal sin," I countered.

"Well, he doesn't think so, but I sure do," she snapped at me as we walked by the end of the line.

"I'll tell you what," I responded calmly. "I'll bet you a hundred dollars they all go to heaven."

"What makes you so damn sure of that?" she challenged with a noticeable degree of smugness. "It's easy. They've been to hell already," I explained with certainty.

The remainder of my last day on this ward was spent less eventfully, but equally as reflective on the role religion plays in how we treat our fellow human beings.

Driving my car off the campus and re-entering the real world, I felt intensely dichotomous emotions impacting my level of consciousness. Relieved that I no longer had to be a party to such horrific experiences, I nonetheless realized that the awareness of this aspect of our human condition gave rise to an unsettling urge for rectification. It was time to get back to campus and find out what my colleagues had experienced on their field trips.

Classroom control, while an important element within special education, rarely poses a problem at the university level of instruction. Confronted with twenty-five psychologically distraught students eager to vent their reaction, Blatt

60

did well to help his charges channel their emotionality appropriately. Listening reflectively, he absorbed immense levels of anger and frustration with a system whose concern for human ecology appeared nonexistent.

It took nearly a week to de-program the entire group as we shared horror stories observed in a variety of state operated facilities serving the mentally retarded and mentally ill. Vivid, first-hand depictions of electroshock therapy stunned the listeners, and made the pain of our visitations appear less traumatic. Horror stories abounded during these few days as our anger level dissipated to the point where we were able to proceed further with our learning experiences.

More lectures, films, and guest speakers filled our consciences with additional guilt for being a part of a society that treated some of its members in such a dehumanizing fashion. Day trips to Indian reservations and senior citizen apartment complexes pointed out our nation's penchant for segregating certain groups for convenience sake. We were virtually mobbed by the senior citizens who were desperate for just someone to listen to them. They literally fought over access to us and blocked our path to the elevators when it came time to leave. This type of warehousing struck much closer to home and made the theme of the workshop more strikingly relevant.

Preparing for our next field visit, the choices boiled down to another trip to back ward venues such as we had previously experienced or, for a unique few, the opportunity to visit the institutional equivalent of nirvana. The final chapter of **Christmas in Purgatory** had visually detailed the existence of an alternative to the intensive dehumanization that was so pervasive throughout the document. The Seaside Regional Center, located on the ocean shore of Connecticut, offered an example of how well-intended advocates for the mentally retarded could create settings in which meaningful care could take place for those who we had seen abused in traditional institutions. Unwilling to spend three more days in an environment similar to my first visit and hoping to discover the existence of a service delivery system that held the potential for success, I anxiously signed up to visit the dramatic antithesis of what had been the epitome of our learning experience.

Our trip to Seaside was an experience that was a startling contrast to the visitation of the State School in a wide variety of ways. The beautiful, well kept campus laid out over prime seashore property, eloquently spoke to the commitment of that state to those who they are entrusted with caring for. The buildings were bright and well kept, totally devoid of anything resembling a day room. While there were retardates whose measurable I.Q.'s were similar to those of our initial visit, we saw nothing comparable to a back ward. Indeed, each individual was fully clothed and clean, resulting in strong evidence that human dignity was a high priority in this institutional setting. The frequently observable interactions between staff and clients provided ongoing examples of mutual respect and warm feelings. One of the highlights of my stay was enjoying lunch in a common cafeteria where I shared a table with the Director, one of his staff, and two clients. Our conversation dealt with each of their feelings regarding Seaside, and was a perfect example of the concept of normalization in action.

Creativity abounded within this unique community of caring and concern. Theme weekends throughout the summer were a highlight for all the residents. One such happening was appropriately entitled "Christmas in July," and centered around Santa arriving via a submarine from the local Navy base. As the sub emerged from the water and the Jolly Old Elf stepped out of the hatch, hundreds of residents on the beach reacted joyously to this unique visual and emotional experience.

Another exciting aspect of the Seaside adventure was the supportive community involvement. Numerous young and eager volunteers were consistently seen working with children and adults who thrived on the meaningful individual attention. At the suggestion of a staff member, I drove my car a few miles off the campus to a gas station that had been donated by a local citizen for the purpose of teaching capable residents the skills necessary to work in this field. I had my oil changed and my tank filled up with gasoline as I observed a group of residents, under the direction of an instructor, serve the public cheerfully for over an hour. What a sharp contrast of how these two settings viewed the human potential of the mentally retarded!

Returning to the campus following our stay in the institutional equivalent of the promised land, we were anxious to express our feelings of hope to those whose visits had been once again to those less fortunate. Their tales of human abuse continued unabated, as they detailed, with depressing finality, the horrendous level of malfeasance with which the state responded to its mission to care for and treat those we choose to institutionalize. Our experience, however, was one that allowed us to view the light (albeit glimmering faintly) at the end of the tunnel.

The final week of the workshop was geared toward arriving at some potential courses of action that each of us, or groups of us, might take to rectify the conditions we had born witness to during the preceding month. The individuals within the group had developed a unique kinship and camaraderie that was not unlike that experienced during a tour of duty in the military. Many of these friendships have continued on personally and professionally for over two decades.

Dr. Blatt carefully directed our thinking, as we suggested potential methods for impacting on public policy regarding the future of state institutions. Dramatic change was our immediate goal and ultimate closure of back wards was a necessity. Community residences for thousands of retardates who would be removed from institutional settings became our long term goal. Little did we realize during that week in August of 1970 that each of these wishes would become reality.

Reentry into the day-to-day world following the

workshop was a slow process as the echoes of the experience continued to dwell in my conscience. In the early fall, I signed up to testify at a hearing of the State Legislature's Select Committee on Mental and Physical Handicaps. Reasoning that this group had both the responsibility for and the potential to alter present institutional conditions, I eagerly entered the legislative chambers and mounted the rostrum. Flashing through my mind were snapshots of the barbaric treatment I had witnessed such a short time before.

Cognizant of the need to get the assembled senators' and assemblymens' attention, I began my testimony by asserting, "If William Shakespeare were here before you today, he would strongly suggest that 'something is rotten in the State of New York.'" It worked perfectly, and I held their rapt attention for the next twenty minutes while graphically detailing the magnitude of degradation being perpetrated on a daily basis within our state institutions. As I talked, it was apparent that the legislators' uneasiness was beginning to grow. At the conclusion, one assemblyman spoke up and proposed that had Shakespeare been here he would have said, "the man protesteth too much."

"Assemblyman," I responded, "you represent one of the most affluent areas of New York State. Were you living today as a resident of one of our state institutions, you would assert 'the man speaketh out too little.'"

Leaving the building that day, I was approached by numerous parents of children in state facilities who thanked me profusely for having testified. As satisfying as the experience was, I often wondered whether such testimony had much impact on the behavior of legislators. Some five years after that hearing, one of my colleagues from the workshop visited the state capital with me. We walked into the office of the Select Committee and he asked the secretary if they had copies of testimony from previous years. Giving an affirmative response she asked the name of the person whose statement he wished to review. Upon hearing my name, she immediately responded, "Oh yes, he was the man

64

who began by quoting Shakespeare. I know just where that file is." Maybe the system does work, after all.

That winter, as we began practicing for our recreational basketball league, one of my teammates approached me one evening seeking my advice. Earlier that week his wife, the sister of a close friend of mine, had given birth to a child with severe retardation and multiple physical handicaps. Knowing of my experiences, they were inquiring about the practicability of placing their baby in a state institution. Uncomfortable in being placed in this position, I merely detailed for him my observations and the strong negative emotional impact such facilities had upon those who had studied with me. I then inquired about what advice their obstetrician gave them.

"He says just to treat the baby the same way we would treat a normal infant, and she will die quietly," I was told by the father.

Stunned by the callousness of this suggestion, it nonetheless underlined the total lack of alternatives for parents who found themselves facing this grave moral dilemma. It also reenforced my beliefs regarding the shallow nature of the medical profession's creativity when dealing with the area of disability. The director of every facility for the mentally retarded and the mentally ill that we visited had initials MD after his or her name.

On New Year's Eve, I had the opportunity to meet the baby for the first time. Her parents brought her to a party being held at her aunt and uncle's house. Other than an atypical skin color, there was little or no evidence of abnormality to the untrained observer. She spent the evening in an upstairs bedroom while the revelers partied the night away downstairs in the family room. On New Year's Day, I received a phone call informing me that sometime during the early morning hours the baby had succumbed to the impact of her multiple physical problems, just as her doctor had predicted. My New Year's resolution for 1971 was easy to arrive at, and I joined the battle to develop meaningful support systems for the parents of exceptional children.

Coming out of the Workshop on Human Abuse was the creation at the university of an advocacy system known as the Center on Human Policy. This agency was formed to provide support and counsel for those who assist the disabled. The Center was carefully guided by Dr. Blatt's beliefs in the dignity of every human being. The Center became a rallying point for those who desired to change the nature of institutions, as well as for those who wished to facilitate new legislation dealing with the education of disabled children. Today the Center continues to flourish as a living monument to Blatt's dreams for a better society for exceptional individuals.

I began the summer primarily as a special educator whose professional focus was creating educational alternatives for children. My life was dramatically invaded and a mission with equal importance resulted. The de-institution movement became the second front upon which we now waged social revolution. The impact of that experience upon each of us had profound implications. Knowledge of the conditions existent in these institutions, long hidden from the public at large, made it difficult to sleep peacefully each night. Many an evening I found myself returning to that back ward and standing by George's bedside.

"Hi, my name is Mark. I'm twenty-nine years old, and I won't rest until we clean this place up and get you and your friends the hell out of here."

High on a Hillside

Paradoxically, my first working day following the six week conversion to the cause of de-institutionalization was spent assuming the responsibilities of my first administrative position - creating a brand new school in a residential treatment center. Reflecting on the irony of the situation, it was necessary to separate the distinctions between our society's treatment of the mentally retarded and the historical evolution of our child care system through the concept of orphanages. My experiences as a college senior had left me with a profound respect for the efficacy of residential treatment, and by 1970 creative alternatives for serving children from destructive home environments were still rather limited. I begged Dr. Blatt's forgiveness, and set about my new professional challenge with determination, tempered with the anxiety and caution indigenous to blazing an unfamiliar trail.

Up to this time, my experience as a special educator was entirely with children whose primary handicapping condition was mental retardation. Behavior management within the classroom had never been an issue necessitating any significant amount of my time or energy. Climbing the academic ladder of learning had been a task my students were eager to address and willing to commit themselves to, as long as they saw ongoing success resulting from their efforts.

From this placid and copacetic professional environment, I agreed to venture into an arena that would be replete with heavy dosages of anger, frustration, aggression and resistance to learning. The subtleties of this switch would be as unobtrusive as being sacked by NY Giants' Linebacker Lawrence Taylor. My students had all been thrown out of a large urban school district's special education program - one that at the time had an outstanding national reputation. Their educational dossiers gave graphic testimony as to why they were cut loose from what wished to remain an orderly educational system. The behavioral manifestation of their emotional needs had not been appropriately sublimated to the degree needed by their unfortunate teachers and building principals. As a result, they were now my responsibility.

When I arrived at Hillside Children's Center, it had been serving children from the Rochester area for well over a century. It began, like many other such institutions, as a facility whose mission it was to provide housing and nurturing for young children without parents. In those days such children were considered to be orphans and their care was usually the result of well-intended church groups throughout the nation. As a result, their budgets were small, staffing patterns limited,and for the children,there was some degree of stigma attached to being raised there.

After a major fire destroyed the original Center, the new campus was developed on a beautiful site overlooking an attractive area of Rochester. Contiguous to superb and multi-faceted public parks, the center was close by a wide range of services conducive to constructively supporting the primary needs of growing children. Seven cottages (five for boys, two for girls) housed over ninety children with a rotating childcare staff working hard to provide a homelike environment.

Following World War II, the nature of the children being served in orphanages throughout the Northeast began to change. More and more, the type of youngster being placed in these institutions manifested varying degrees of emotional problems. Marital breakups, child abuse, drug and alcohol problems became contributing factors to the deteriorating family lives these children had experienced prior to placement. Departments of Social Service and Family Courts were requesting a change of mission on the part of child care service providers in order to respond to this ever growing problem. Public tax dollars, as a result, began to flow into such facilities in the form of per diem rates for service and additional, better-trained staff were employed. The term "residential treatment center" became the title of many of these more modern facilities. Psychiatrists, clinical psychologists, and eventually special educators entered the domain that was once the sole purview of nuns, child care workers and social workers.

During the 1960s, Hillside was slowly moving from meeting the needs of less troubled youth to gearing up for the challenges that seriously disturbed children presented. Toward the end of that turbulent decade, the Board of Directors wisely decided to employ as their Executive Director an experienced administrator from New England, Mr. James Cotter, M.S.W. Cotter had previously provided competent leadership for smaller, similar agencies and brought with him to Rochester a wide array of professional skills, combined with the vision necessary to officiate over institutional transformation. Key among his skills was the ability to convince a wealthy, conservative Board to allow him to take the risks inherent in bringing about the changes required to help Hillside catch up with their more progressive competitors. One of his first moves in this direction was the decision to create a Campus School to meet the special educational needs of those residents who were no longer able to attend public schools. To this end, upon permission from the Board, was posted the position of Director of Education.

Having put in seven enjoyable years in the public sector with significant satisfaction, I was intrigued when the guidance counselor at Walt Disney Elementary showed me the posting for this position. Having little idea of what the job entailed, my eagerness to assume a leadership position piqued my curiosity. Recognizing the impact of leaving the public schools might have on my future career path, I nonetheless contacted Cotter to discuss my potential for filling this administrative role.

During the interview, he clearly articulated his rationale for creating this new component to the Center's array of services. Cotter carefully detailed the nature and needs of the children to be served, and made no bones about the challenges presented by this responsibility. Being the first educator, special or otherwise, on their leadership team would be a major test of administrative skills. On the other hand, few professionals ever have the opportunity to create their own school from scratch (albeit for children with severe emotional problems).

The next day at school was spent attempting to assess the positive and negative factors involved with assuming this new position. Leaving a job that had been such a fine learning experience could be scary, but my mind kept returning to the memories of my nine months at the House of Providence. The beauty and exhilaration of that period in my life had never left me. Kids like Jonathan were still in even greater need for alternatives, and if given a chance, I could create one of my own for them. That evening, when the phone rang and Cotter offered me the job, it didn't take long for me to accept. At age twenty-eight, I had just assumed responsibility for developing a meaningful educational program for the most troubled children in a major Northeastern city. My high level of excitement was appropriately tempered by doses of self-doubt that such a challenge intrinsically emits.

During the interview process, it had been determined, that at the outset there would be two classes in the campus school, and my role would temporarily be that of a teaching principal. In addition, I had convinced the Executive Director that since our students had been unable to benefit from public school, the salary we paid for teachers should in turn be in excess of what they would earn in the public sector. This was an extremely unique concession on his part, but it was critical to the development of our school.

After hanging up the telephone, I immediately placed one of the most important calls of my career. Given the nature of the challenge that lay ahead, it was most evident, that for us to succeed, it was necessary to recruit the best educator available. Having taught in four separate school buildings over the previous seven years, I had observed a wide variety of regular and special educators in action. Even though I hadn't worked with her for three years, I never lost contact with the one professional who could handle teaching in this setting.

Jackie Deck had taught in the classroom next to mine in a suburban school building for two years and her skill with reluctant learners always amazed me. She was consistently able to meet the nurturing needs of her young charges by expecting them to respond to her academic and behavioral demands. The success that they experienced proved to be reward enough for their efforts, but, in addition, she always provided positive reinforcement, creating a happy, supportive environment within her classroom. Barely five feet tall, she created a high level of teacher presence that constantly reassured her students that caring and growth were abundantly available as needed.

My first administrative decision was to offer Jackie the opportunity to be my colleague and partner in the development of the Campus School. In retrospect, it seems terribly ironic that the first decision I made turned out to be far and away the best. I was appropriately thrilled when she accepted this sizable challenge. The validity of my selection was reinforced many years later, when in her first year of teaching in that state, Jackie was selected as Florida's Teacher of the Year.

With Jackie as my teaching partner, my level of optimism in embarking upon this exciting endeavor began to soar. She would take the group of six youngsters ages seven through ten, and I would concentrate my energies upon a similar sized group of eleven to fourteen year olds. The fact that it was also incumbent upon me to perform all of the requisite administrative duties consistent with developing such a program didn't appear to be much of a concern at that juncture. Then again, I hadn't even met with the students we would be serving.

71

Provided with a list of the children we would be responsible for in September, the two of us spent the month of June visiting with the teachers throughout the city school district who had last attempted to provide meaningful instruction for them. Each of these meetings resulted in our being bombarded with a litany of grievous offenses against the good order of the classroom perpetrated by our children. It seemed like every teacher displayed significant relief in knowing that he or she would never see this student again and each building principal used the word "commitment" when discussing my new assignment. I was never quite sure just how they meant that.

In an attempt to combat the apprehension brought on by these visits to the past battlefields of our young charges, we decided to also visit the campus school programs of residential treatment centers in Buffalo and Syracuse. Both of these programs had been functioning for quite a while and their respective Directors of Education were gracious and eager to help their fledgling colleague in need. From these visits developed both personal and professional relationships that have been highly productive over the past twenty years. Having this opportunity to see first hand how effectively such programs can operate was highly reassuring. Observing teachers working in an orderly classroom and discussing keys to the successful interface between the educational and residential components of the facility provided me with vital information upon which to develop policies for our still embryonic school program. Suggestions for curriculum and behavior management techniques provided both Jackie and myself with invaluable guidance. For as eager and enthusiastic as we were over accepting this challenge, the bottom line still remained that neither one of us had ever provided educational services within the classroom to students categorized as emotionally disturbed.

Provided with a turn of the century vintage two story building, it was my duty to transform this space into an appealing environment conducive to learning. After visiting other such schools and doing research in the public library, the task became picking out carpeting, desks, equipment, room dividers, and instructional supplies for the upcoming school year. We decided that one of the two classrooms would be equipped with a one-way viewing mirror so that visitors might witness the wonders we would be working within. I decided Jackie's room should be the one so equipped.

Interior decorating was certainly not my forte, but most people respected my claim of color blindness as a logical explanation. However, in retrospect, we could have better thought out some areas. This I learned in a rather dramatic fashion one day when confronted by an extremely angry twelve year old student who was street smart and very well-built. Having had enough of what I was putting down, he decided to exit through the front door of the school in a climactic manner. Slamming the door in my face he punctuated his displeasure with me by kicking the door with the back of his heel. Unfortunately, it was a glass door which immediately shattered, with the remnants thereof falling all over me. As angry as I might have become over the incident, it provided me with much better direction for my next venture into the decorating business.

A high priority during this preparation period was getting to know the kids who lived on "the Hill," especially those who would be coming to the campus school. We were realistically concerned that there would be a degree of stigma attached to having to attend school on the grounds. With ninety percent of the children attending local public schools, some bitterness might emerge. Relationship building became the thrust of many of my activities, as I grew to know my students through recreational activities and visits to their cottages. Their hesitation to develop a degree of closeness toward me was tempered by their curiosity about what their new school might be like. Accentuating the positive, my goal was to convince them our school was to be an opportunity, not a punishment, and that I was really looking forward to working with them.

During this rapport building and public relations stage, I decided to join a large group of youngsters on a day long field trip to a state park some fifty miles south of the city. The informality of this occasion would offer me the opportunity to see a high percentage of our population in a stimulating activity conducted by staff who had worked with them for some time. As the bus wound its way along country roads, it became apparent to me that not all of our kids were tough, street-wise victims of parental neglect. A small proportion of the group was made up of children with severe emotional disturbance. Many of them had previously been residents of state-operated psychiatric facilities. While the tougher kids failed to even acknowledge the existence of this other group, I couldn't help but wonder how the mix must impact on programming and treatment.

Upon reaching the park, the urchins quickly changed into their swim wear to swim in the cool brook that constituted the highlight of this recreational area. Sitting on a ledge overlooking the brook, I carefully observed this excited mass as they frolicked joyfully in a most normal manner. Suddenly, my attention was drawn to a remote area of the water where two of our adolescents who had recently been discharged from psychiatric facilities were sitting comfortably. From my vantage point, it appeared they were deeply engrossed in a conversation that resulted in frequent smiles and refreshing laughter. How nice it is that they have found each other, I thought to myself, and it might be the first boy-girl relationship either of them had experienced. Wading out in such a manner to avoid arousing their curiosity, I cautiously inched closer to them, until, when within earshot, I also sat down in the water facing the other direction. It was only then that I realized that,while they had been facing each other only inches apart, these two unfortunate souls had each been conducting, for the past ten minutes, a conversation with himself and herself. The trip turned out to be every bit the learning experience I had hoped for.

Attending weekly meetings of the administrative staff during the summer taught me much about how the agency functioned. As the only person other than the recreation director who did not possess a master's degree in social work (MSW) it was sometimes awkward for me as I attempted to master the jargon while psyching out the value system that prevailed within the organization. My colleagues were friendly but careful to reserve judgement about the importance of the school in the overall scheme of things on the Hill. Aware of the likelihood of my marching to a different drummer, many of the social work staff were overly cautious when approaching me to discuss the goals of the school or the needs of individual children. For some reason, I felt like a missionary whose job it was to facilitate conversion on foreign turf. Quickly, the realization hit me that it would be imperative to develop a high quality communication system with the Executive Director so that at all times he was both cognizant and supportive of what we were trying to accomplish within the school program. As others witnessed his commitment to make the school an effective component of the overall service delivery system of the agency, they would appreciate the wisdom of his decision to create such an entity and become supporters of our efforts. However, we well recognized that the key to our success would be how effectively we could change our students behavior and rate of learning which in turn would impact their self-esteem and bear witness to the value of our mission. September couldn't come soon enough that year for Jackie and me.

While, overall, the opening of the campus school was relatively uneventful, the early fall brought me into a state of deep appreciation of the noticeable differences between working with those whose primary disability was mental retardation and children whose level of emotional disturbance required they be placed in residential facilities. Those children at Hillside, whose level of need dictated their placement in the on-grounds school, were of such a nature that the behavioral components of their disability were vividly manifest. Abusive and neglectful parenting resulted in a total distrust of adults and an unwillingness to develop a relationship that might ultimately become hurtful. The emotional scars incurred during their young lives were slow to heal, and even the most well meaning attempts to be supportive were oftentimes met with resistance or hostility. Only those who possess high levels of inner stubbornness could possibly survive in this emotional equivalent of hand-to-hand combat. During such conflict, the adult must constantly recognize that the barrage of venom viciously spewed forth was at best intended for an adult from the child's past who had most likely deserved such treatment. Those who personalized such tirades quickly sought out alternative employment.

On the other hand, it was imperative that Jackie and I quickly establish the normative acceptable behavior within the school so that such limits were apparent to students and staff alike. Each of us had a teacher aide functioning within the classroom and they were crucial in assisting us to maintain our level of expectations. In addition, much effort was spent in communicating these norms to social work, recreation, and cottage staff who formed the other critical components of the treatment team. Without their support and willing involvement, we weren't going to last very long in developing our fledgling school program.

My class consisted of eight intermediate to junior high level students whose prior educational involvement was markedly under-productive. Those who possessed reasonable levels of academic skill demonstrated a distinct unwillingness to apply such ability relative to the learning process. Others utilized a wide variety of behavioral outbursts to mask their inability to learn and the frustration concomitant with that condition. Grouping for instruction became at best an impossibility, and individualizing instruction became necessary for survival. Each day brought another battle to increase time on-task and to lessen the amount of time and effort spent on behavior management.

Tim was a wiry twelve year old boy who had ridden the merry-go-round of foster homes prior to placement on the Hill. Possessing a number of likable qualities, he nonetheless harbored a high degree of resentment toward his last set of foster parents. When Tim found one of their other children dead in the clothes dryer, they accused him of having put the child in there. Carrying this accusation on his young shoulders, Tim had little or no interest in academic pursuits.

On the other hand, Tim did have a great interest in football and often wore his Pop Warner uniform to school. Observing this phenomenon, it occurred to me that we might be able to gain entry to his brain through his helmet. Introducing into the classroom a number of sports magazines highlighting football, I noticed he would sit for hours thumbing through them with a high level of interest. One morning he opened the door I had so patiently been waiting for.

"Mr. Costello, I want to write a book about football, he said. "Will you help me?"

"You bet I will," I replied while trying to restrain my enthusiasm. For the next ten weeks, the two of us worked on his book. Learning to spell and to write appropriately was now a tolerable activity. We taught math by including simulated football games and statistics into his journal. Art activities were a natural to spruce up the quality of his literary effort. The history of the game related to current events of those times allowed us to expand our curriculum even wider. Tim had taught me the subtleties of reaching reluctant learners and the experience was more enjoyable than any half-time show I've ever witnessed.

Susan was an attractive twelve year old girl who was the sole representative of her gender in our school. She had reportedly been the victim of sexual abuse and as a result withdrew significantly from the real world. In order to facilitate this she claimed to be visually impaired to the degree that she insisted she was unable to perform any task requiring sight. One psychologist diagnosed her as the victim of "hysterical blindness." Needless to say, her condition created serious ramifications instructionally within the classroom. Having no skills whatsoever in the area of teaching the visually impaired and becoming more skeptical each day of the validity of her assertions, I decided to fall back and rely on the only card I had left in my hand - stubbornness.

"But, I can't see the paper," she alleged.

"I don't care if you can see it or not, just write down the correct answers," I countered.

By increasing both the positive and negative consequences for accomplishing each task, I soon discovered that whether she could see or not, Susan could get her work done and grow academically. Stubbornness and determination proved to be critical qualities to draw upon as an educator of the emotionally disturbed.

Tony was an enigmatic child whose potential for creating frustration for those adults who worked with him was unlimited. A tall, handsome eleven year old, he was mature far beyond his chronological age. When he was cooperative, Tony could be a joy to be around, and someone any teacher would love to have as a member of the class. But instantaneously his mood and attitude would change dramatically, without provocation, and he would begin to verbally abuse whoever he was working with by threatening them with all forms of physical violence. Fortunately, Tony never followed through on his threats, but it would, on occasion, take an adult up to an hour to dissipate his anger, primarily because there had been no logical causation for his sudden change in character.

Needing to be physically restrained during these sometimes dramatic outbursts, Tony became quite a management problem. Aware of the charismatic and talented young boy lurking just below the surface of the hostile aggressive youth I was interacting with helped to keep me on-task, but, at the same time, created excessive levels of frustration. One day, while holding Tony during one of these unanticipated episodes, I stumbled upon the secret to restoring his more appropriate personality. I noticed that when gripping him by the wrists to protect myself, his anger would go on unabated for long periods of time, but as I moved my hands up his arms, he seemed to appear pacified and began to calm down. It dawned on me that, in this manner, Tony would quickly retreat to being his old lovable self. While being a firm believer in the concept of "any port in a storm," from that day forward I restrained Tony by holding him firmly by the shoulders which would facilitate his redirection in a much more tolerable time-frame, and significantly increase the amount of his instructional involvement. Of all the students we worked with, Tony most poignantly epitomized the roller coaster ride between enjoyment and frustration that was characteristic of teaching children with severe emotional problems.

As the fall semester proceeded, with Jackie doing an outstanding job of teaching the younger class, we gradually established the normative behavior pattern so crucial to the development of the program. Once that was formalized, all new entrants into the program quickly conformed to the expectations held by school staff and things began to run smoothly. Children began to be referred to the agency as a direct result of the school's existence. It soon became readily apparent to all of us on the administrative level that the future of Hillside would be determined by the ability of the on-grounds school to absorb greater numbers of children with severe emotional needs and multifarious learning problems.

Few educational historians have accurately described the impact that our country's military involvement in southeast Asia had upon the landscape of education in general, and special education, in particular, during the 1960s and 1970s. Nowhere was this influence felt more dramatically than at residential treatment centers such as ours. While public school special educators had for many years received preferred draft status because of the Kennedy Administration's interest in programs for children with disabilities, Hillside, and agencies like it, became the setting to which judges assigned conscientious objectors to perform their "alternative service" obligations. This phenomenon resulted in the center employing a significant number of young males in their early 20s, most of whom held college degrees, to work with our difficult population of children.

While, for the most part, the great majority of these child-care workers and teacher aides possessed a high level of social consciousness, their commitment to meeting the needs of children and the goals of the agencies showed a high level of variability. Some CO's arrived on the Hill with the attitude that beating the "corrupt system" was an ongoing battle, and that putting forth as little effort as was necessary to survive was a good way of peacefully protesting their adjudicated fate. The majority, however, realized the urgency of our mission and gave of their energy in the effort to present positive role models for children who had previously found in adults only hostility and unpredictability. While frequently rejecting their long hair and style of dress, the children did respond favorably to young adults who would listen to them and respond in a consistent manner to their sometimes erratic behavior. For many of these young men, this experience became a discovery of a meaningful career that would ultimately impact positively on the social fabric of our nation. Scattered throughout New York State today, in vital leadership positions in education and human services, are numerous members of this group who, were it not for the military conflict of that era, would undoubtedly have pursued other avenues of employment.

As fall wore on, the patterns of responsibility in my role began to emerge, and the importance of maintaining emotional equilibrium became more apparent. Creativity, common sense, humor, and determination became wells requiring frequent tapping. Each Thursday became a test of my ability to cope with psychological intensity. While the students seemed to pick that day to express their most deeply held frustrations, the afternoon in-take meetings with the agency hierarchy ultimately strained one's tolerance for empathic pain. Reading and discussing volumes of referral information on four or five of the area's most unwanted and abused children, most of whom needed our help desperately, became a highly depressing experience. Working with them once they were in residence was considerably easier, and, in the majority of cases, the written word proved woefully inadequate in providing a balanced picture of the child whose care and treatment we would be accepting responsibility for. By giving the children the benefit of the doubt on close calls, we rarely ended up with a youngster we couldn't positively impact upon.

As the amount of time allocated for administrative duties grew, my awareness of being the educator in the world of social workers became more acute. Humor helped me deal with my name being the only one on our stationery not followed by the letters MSW. Attempting to insert some frivolity into the beginning of our weekly in-take meeting, I told my colleagues, "I just heard a new radio station on my way to work - WMSW."

Accepting the veracity of my assertion with excitement, they were unhappy to hear that this unique station offered, "No news, no music - just a lot of static."

In addition to being a classroom teacher and the school principal, I also conducted the physical education classes each week. What passed for a gymnasium was a small area in the basement of one of the cottages with baskets at either end. Running up and down the court never posed a problem, but the out-of-bounds was a concrete wall which made some games exciting. Trying to orchestrate each game so that the ego needs of the competitors were constantly taken into consideration was a challenge to my athletic skills and ability to manipulate the surface behavior of children. A twenty minute game could feel like the Boston Marathon. Occasionally, when mental health needs dictated, Friday afternoon would be devoted to a game of roller hockey between students and staff. Riding your favorite student (or teacher) of the week into the wall with a clean check created a level of catharsis unmatched by any other area of the curriculum. At the conclusion, everyone shook hands and left the gym with better feelings about each other than when they had entered.

Civic organizations have an outstanding record of accomplishment for providing enjoyable experiences for underprivileged children. I am confident that the Junior Chamber of Commerce had only the best intentions when they offered to take our students in their own cars to Niagara Falls for an outing that included a wide variety of disabled children throughout western New York State. I tried my best to explain the nature of our pupils and the management issues that could result from an over stimulating experience, but this group of eager young men seemed undaunted by my admonitions. With three students in each car chaperoned by two Jaycees, the odds appeared favorable.

Arriving an hour and a half later at the historical haven for honeymooners, one of the drivers requested my help in convincing the boys in his car that they should not make obscene gestures to passing police cars along the way. Reality was setting in.

Entering the Aquarium, many of our charges were upset to discover that the front rows of seats above the dolphin tank were already filled with children with mental retardation from another school. Wishing to move into closer seating, one of our students decided to toss the hat of one of these prior arrivals into the tank full of dolphins in hope that the victim would vacate his seat while seeking to regain his cap. Needless to say, this caused quite a stir but peace was eventually restored just as another one of our cherubs was detected trying to break the glass in a small tank encased in the wall which housed an electric eel. It seems his curiosity had gotten the better of him and he just wanted to touch this unique fish.

A visit to the Falls itself necessitated each Jaycee holding firmly the hand of his buddy for the day, and the awesome nature of the spectacle seemed to mitigate against additional risk taking behavior. Growing consistently more frazzled, our hosts then took us to the space needle, at whose apex awaited a revolving restaurant. The students quickly devoured their lunch so that they might more deeply probe the mechanical workings of this unique building, as well as the elevator that had brought us to its summit. We quickly rounded up each carload and sent them on their way back to the Hill in order to preserve one of nature's wonders. As we drove up the driveway, I fully appreciated the value of the tight structure we were able to provide these children with, and wished the Jaycees could come back to see us on our home field. Somehow, I knew they probably wouldn't be making such a request.

As our school grew in numbers, the need to interview and select skillful personnel became critical to our success. As a private school, which at that early stage of our evolution had yet to apply for State Education Department approval, we were afforded the luxury of employing uncertified teachers. With this flexibility, we were able to choose from a wide pool of candidates whose motivation to work with troublesome children was extremely high. Their post-secondary preparation was in a variety of disciplines, but it was obvious that both their levels of energy and charisma were of the highest order. The ability of these young adults to relate to children in an academic arena, where failure had been their past practice, was exciting to be a part of. The enthusiasm and determination they brought daily into the classroom signaled hope and potential for success to such a degree that their students eagerly attacked the curriculum they presented. In fact, the most trying period of each school day revolved around persuading the children to leave the school building after dismissal; such were the emotional ties developed between the students and their teacher or teacher aide.

As we grew and created new classes, it was decided that we would try to staff these classrooms in such a manner so as to have both a male and female adult assigned to each group of students. Given the background of our pupils and the difficult family situation they had come out of, we felt that by giving each child the opportunity to relate to a healthy adult image of both sexes would create a more psychologically supportive environment in which to learn. This proved to be a vital asset in the overall psycho-educational milieu that developed within the campus school during the initial stages of its growth.

Faced with a rapid rate of resident referrals for service, soon after the new year opened, I left the classroom to become a full-time administrator. While this transition resulted in mixed feelings on my part (as I recognized it could spell the end of my teaching career), I was anxious about our potential to self-destruct if we grew too quickly without the appropriate structure and support necessary to manage these changes. Coincidentally, while this change was taking place, we also developed the need for a full-time teacher who could also teach physical education in a more meaningful way to our energetic youngsters. Into this breach stepped an old friend from my high school days who held a bachelor's degree in physical education and nearly ten years experience as a recreation director at some of the toughest playgrounds in Rochester. Knowledgeable about street kids and their survival behaviors, Terry Clar joined our team at this critical juncture and was instrumental in providing a higher level of structure and discipline within the total program on the Hill. Relating closely with the recreation staff and the cottage personnel, Terry helped set a tone of cooperation and communication which brought a strong team effort to fruition in meeting the total treatment needs of our clientele. His presence on our educational staff made each of us more confident in our ability to deal with the high level of spontaneous behavior management that was such a part of our professional lives. The children loved and respected Terry for his knowledge of their needs, concern for their best interest, and fairness in dealing with each of them.

Functioning now as a full-time principal allowed me to develop a new type of relationship with the students. With Terry on board, Jackie doing her usual exceptional job in the classroom, and a young enthusiastic staff at my command, we had all the ingredients necessary to deliver a high quality program. With the normative behavioral expectations well articulated and accepted by the children, student discipline became considerably less of an issue. As new students entered the program on an almost weekly basis, it was my responsibility to see that they made a comfortable adjustment into their new classroom setting. Having read their life stories nearly a month prior to their arrival, I was acutely aware of the psychological damage they had incurred prior to placement. On the other hand, my knowledge of the havoc they had spread throughout the traditional school system convinced me that they should quickly be lead to understand the uniqueness of their new school.

In an attempt to communicate both the seriousness of our purpose and our respect for each child as an individual, I held an entrance interview with each new student. Posturing myself in such a manner to convey both authority and understanding, my short, yet serious message usually concluded with the following admonition.

"My young friend, you know why you are here and I know why you're here. Let's not try to fool each other. This could well be your last chance to turn your school life around and we have the people here who can help you make that happen."

Usually, by this stage of our discussion, the student would begin to make eye contact with me and drop the tough guy facade present from the outset of the meeting. After explaining the consequences of both positive and negative behavior in a satisfactory manner, the final line I used to gain closure went something to this effect.

"I've enjoyed talking with you and hope you benefit from your time in our school. Remember the school colors are black and blue and our alma mater is Cher's latest hit, "Gypsies, Tramps, and Thieves." If you need to come to my office again, it might not be under such friendly terms as this, so do a good job. Let's go meet your new classmates."

Proud of our consistently improving educational service, and wishing to develop a working relationship with key personnel from the city school district, I invited two of my professional colleagues to visit. The Assistant Superintendent and Director of Special Education paid a visit one afternoon soon after dismissal. Having been a student of both of them while taking graduate courses for certification purposes, I was most anxious to impress them with the quality of our creation. We walked slowly through the building while I proudly articulated the finer points of our specialized educational program. I was soon chagrined by what appeared to be a major fight breaking out in the school library which we allowed the recreational staff to utilize after school hours. Not wanting to appear unable to deal with crisis, I kept talking calmly to my guests as I physically carried various combatants out the side door. Unfortunately, things escalated as tempers flared to even higher levels, and soon my visitors joined in the fracas as the three of us helped the recreation staff restore order to our premises. With a knowing look of understanding, these two experienced special education leaders pledged their support to assist us in making the campus school a viable alternative for area children. In reality, our ability to flourish as an appropriate center for learning would relieve the city school district of the need to educate many of its most difficult students.

As we became gradually more established in the educational community, a rather unsettling phenomenon began to occur. The principal of the neighboring public elementary school (where large numbers of our residents attended) took it upon herself to call my office and request that I come to her office to take those children she desired to suspend back to our campus. Trying to explain to her that this activity was not a legitimate function of my role as Director of Education was less than successful. Subsequently, she called me one afternoon to indignantly inform me that I must arrive, post haste, in her office to pick up an eleven year old boy from one of our cottages who had the audacity to return to school after lunch with a squirrel he had met during his journey from the Hill. In a rather uncooperative mood, I inquired as to what problems the squirrel might be causing within her school. She admitted there were no particular problems at the moment, but she was sure there would be some soon. I suggested a creative teacher might utilize this opportunity to some positive results, were an appropriate cage available. Ultimately unsuccessful, I arrived at the school to find the boy and his squirrel sitting quietly in the office.

"Let me guess, a three day suspension for the boy and the death sentence for the squirrel?" She missed the humor in my question and the three of us returned to the campus without further incident.

Eventually, the suspension rate within her school became intolerable, and it became necessary to stem this flow of injustice. In response to her next request for help, I inquired as to whether or not she kept records of those students who were suspended from school. When she answered affirmatively, it was time to spring my trap.

"Great," I countered, "would you be willing to help me?"

"Help you with what?" she probed.

"I'm doing doctoral level research at Syracuse University and my study has to do with the difference in rates of school suspension between two groups of children - those who live at home with their parents, and those who live in residential placement. It seems like your school would be perfect for gathering such data. How about it?"

She never called my office again, and on those extremely rare occasions where one of our kids got into trouble, his caseworker told me it was for legitimate reasons.

The Christmas season in residential treatment facilities is always filled with deeply mixed emotions. While the majority of our society pauses to reflect upon those aspects of their life that bring joy and a spirit of giving, the children cared for in settings such as the Hill are overcome with feelings of ambivalence. Hopeful that they might someday be a component member of a well functioning family unit, the children still feel the pain of their most recent attempt at fulfilling this dream. Those of us who worked with them eagerly shared that hope, and tried as best we could to elicit optimism where the odds seemed prohibitive. The month of December brought with it levels of anxiety that made planning for holiday festivities difficult to indulge in.

The highlight of the Yuletide season was the annual Christmas pageant held in Eastman Hall, which was named after the Rochester philanthropist who developed the camera. The building, which was where all religious events and civic meetings were conducted, stood in the center of the campus. The Glee Club rehearsed extensively in preparation for the concert, to which all parents, board members, and benefactors were invited. For many of these well meaning people, it was an event that brought both pleasure and satisfaction for the role they played in making Hillside the fine facility it was. For some of the children, however, it was a depressing and sometimes traumatic experience.

Aware that all of the parents were invited, the children assembled on the stage dressed in robes fitting the occasion. Well scrubbed and appropriately groomed, the members of the Glee Club appeared as angelic as the circumstances would allow. Singing Christmas carols was certainly not the forte of this group, but they were willing to reach a little to make their parents proud and, hopefully, motivate their parents to allow them to return home. As the program began, smiles broke out upon the faces of many of the children as they made eye contact with their parents. The warm feeling that seeing this generated among the staff soon turned to anxiety as a handful of children visually searched the audience for family members who never arrived. At the completion of the concert, when warm embraces were exchanged, we quickly found ourselves running to those who on this special occasion needed us more than at any time during the year.

Decision making and policy formulation in a school designed to serve emotionally disturbed children needed to reflect the unique nature of our clientele. Every day new problems and atypical issues seemed to surface in such a manner that our problem solving skills would be severely tested. Such was the case when Larry, a fourteen year old boy, joined our student body during late winter of our first year. When his social worker explained to me that he was encopretic, it held little significance. When she explained that as a result of this disorder, Larry expressed displeasure by filling his pants, the impact of her earlier precaution hit home.

Soon after joining the program, Larry's quiet, yet deadly behavior resulted in the need to call a faculty meeting for the purpose of designing a new policy. It was quickly decided that when Larry's "behavior" odoriferously overwhelmed the classroom environment, he would be sent to his cottage to clean up and change his clothes. Only after a call from the cottage worker to the principal would he be considered for re-entry into the class. While that part of the policy development came easy, the remaining question centered around the issue of which staff member should give Larry the order to leave the school. Should it be the teacher aide, the classroom teacher, or the Director of Education?

After a short period of group deliberation, and with the knowledge that expedience was critical in carrying out this mission, we arrived at the following policy.

"You smell him, you tell him."

During my two year tenure on the Hill, rarely did a

day go by where important learning experiences weren't abundant. It always amazed me that the characteristics of these children, which had turned off their parents and teachers in the real world, appeared to rally people who worked at the center around them. Whenever staff from the Hill congregated, invariably the conversation centered around individual children and their needs. What was it about them that inspired advocacy and determination from such a varied population of young adults? I tested this observation with staff from numerous other residential treatment centers and found it to be universally true. Whatever the reason, this ironic phenomenon is critical to the efficacy of agencies such as Hillside.

Many times, particularly when reflecting upon my summer in Purgatory, I would find myself asking the all too obvious question. "Why do we think the best environment for a child with severe emotional problems is in an institutional setting surrounded by one hundred other children with similar or more severe problems?" The incongruity of this dilemma never ceased to amaze me, but as I observed repeated success stories resulting from our model of service delivery it was difficult to cultivate skepticism. To make matters even more complex, we surprisingly discovered that when we sent our children to summer camps for normal functioning peers, not a one of them was sent home because of his or her behavior. Modeling of appropriate social skills seemed to be well within their grasp, as long as a good time would be the end result.

During our second year, Hillside began to flourish under the leadership of Jim Cotter. As an agency, we created a much fuller continuum of services for troubled children. Over a fifteen month period, we developed a series of aftercare alternatives including group homes and expanded foster home settings. At the same time, many of our campus school students began to demonstrate their readiness to return to the public education system. As we witnessed their academic and behavioral growth, the question quickly changed. "Did the local public schools have in place a support system that would facilitate the return of our students in such a manner that success would be predictable?"

Uneasy with the answer to that question, in early spring I visited the newly appointed principal of the school to which our students would be assigned. Aware that one of our group homes was being established across the street from her building, and having housed special education classes in other schools she had led, she was more than willing to explore how we could work cooperatively to support this transition. We decided that what we would do was for me to assign one of my staff who had worked extensively with these particular children to serve as a resource room teacher in her school. The students would be assigned to regular classrooms and would receive supplemental instruction and psychological support from someone they knew and trusted. In order to avoid this service becoming over identified with children from the Hill, and wishing to gain the support of the classroom teachers, I agreed that regular students from the school population could also utilize this instructional support as needed. The model worked well beyond our expectations, and a second one was soon established at the local junior high school. These were the first two resource rooms in the city school district, and it was the success of those students who had been dismissed earlier by the district who made it possible.

As the school and agency grew together and experienced mutual successes, the drive for perfection began to create an aura of excitement in working there. Friendly competition between administrative colleagues was carefully orchestrated in such a manner as to insure a high level of productivity. Our Board of Directors became swept up in the invigorating wave of enthusiasm that pervaded the agency, and eagerly gave thumbs up to any proposal that held potential merit for children. For those youngsters who were fortunate enough to be recipients of the Hill's services, it was a great opportunity to rebuild shattered dreams and head down the right track towards success.

The secret to success in residential treatment centers became abundantly clear to me during this thrilling two year period. Control, communication, and consistency are the three ingredients which allowed us to stop the downward spiral our children had been experiencing. By scheduling their entire twenty-four hour day to limit their potential for unstructured activity, we could insure that their behavior was channeled in the direction of positive outcomes. Staff members throughout the agency communicated verbally, and in written logs, to insure that everyone critical to a child's care and treatment was appraised of what was going on in his or her life at that particular time. These two facets of our treatment methodology ultimately resulted in consistency of adult responses to the needs and behaviors of individual children to the degree that each child, for the first time in his or her development, could predict the outcome of their behavior. This consistency created a sense of security that was at first foreign to the children, but ultimately became the therapeutic element in their pursuit of normalcy.

As effective as we became in meeting the challenges posed by the vast array of uniqueness within our residential population, there was always that one child who would help restore our humility. The most difficult psychological disorder to deal with in settings such as Hillside was far and away masochism. Someone who gains gratification from pain or self-inflicted deprivation can create immeasurable havoc in an environment inhabited with hostile and aggressive peers. I had experience working with such a child at the House of Providence, but he was mild compared to the problems created by a fourteen year old at Hillside named Ernie.

Ernie spent the majority of his waking hours attempting to entice others to respond to him with physical aggression. His idea of a great day was to have peers or staff pound on his body until he was totally black and blue. His mastery of promoting such behavior on the part of others was admirable, and totally frustrating, for those of us who were charged with resisting the temptation. Our growing inability to deal with Ernie's condition resulted in the utilization of rather extreme measures.

One of our cottages had been equipped with a time-out room for out-of-control children who needed a setting in which they could calm down. The room had a supposedly unbreakable window looking out on the campus and a one-way viewing mirror in the door so that a staff member could observe the child inside. Unfortunately, the mirror had been installed backwards, and Ernie was able to see out, while we had no idea what he might be up to. The consequences of this problem became apparent one morning when our Assistant Executive Director was conducting a tour of the campus with a matronly group of wealthy benefactors. They were very impressed with what they were hearing about the quality of our services and the impact their donations were having on our children. The mood of the group suddenly changed when Ernie jumped out of the window of the time-out room clad only in his underwear which he was wearing on his head. Shouting obscenities as he ran across the campus, he made every effort to convince our visitors that there would continue to be a need for future contributions. Unfortunately, Ernie was not around long enough to benefit from their generosity.

Bill joined our teaching staff early in our second year and was assigned to work with our oldest group of students. A tough bunch to handle, he did a fine job of reaching them and brought them along both academically and behaviorally. In his early 30s, Bill had previous experience with emotionally disturbed children, and he drew upon the value of that learning to help his students and his colleagues. Despite performing effectively in the classroom, Bill always seemed to be down on himself and diminished his potential to make meaningful changes in his students. We usually humored him out of these temporary moods, and he shared in many of the staff social activities with enthusiasm. Our closeness as a faculty was always instrumental in assisting each of us over the rough times that were an occupational hazard in this line of work.

During the second year of our serving the residents on the Hill, the State Education Department conducted a program review of the school and provided us with the appropriate accreditation in order to become recipients of state financial assistance. Passing this critical test resulted in financial security for the future and recognition for the program that would insure continuation of student referrals at a consistently rapid rate. This benchmark of credibility was extremely satisfying for Jackie, Terry, and all the staff who had worked so hard to establish this vital alternative for children with emotional problems. Combined with the creation of the resource rooms in the local schools and the growth of our group homes in the community, the campus school was now the hub around which a full array of quality services were revolving. Children with severe emotional problems now had high-quality alternatives available to them, where eight years earlier, only state-operated psychiatric centers existed.

With these successful programs in place, the ability of Hillside to return children to a more normal homelike setting in the community was significantly expedited. Our turn-around time averaged between one and a half to two years, which was highly productive, by any method of measurement. It was a pleasure and an honor to be such a key component on a flourishing team, providing security and success to children who had previously experienced neither.

By late spring, I was once again confronted with a critical career decision. The opportunity arose to attend graduate school full-time at Syracuse University to study special education administration at the expense of the federal government. It would require me to resign my position and sell my new home in the suburbs with no guarantee of future employment. Jackie and Terry were excellent friends and consummate professionals in assisting me to assess the pros and cons of such a move. Leaving "my baby" in the hands of a surrogate leader was a threatening prospect, but the knowledge that the present level of development was so positive was reassuring. Jackie and Terry were strong enough personalities that they would be more than capable of steering the ship on a productive course whoever the new Director might be. With the utmost of confidence in the future of the campus school, I made the decision to ease on down the road to Syracuse.

The following year was a difficult one due to my need to keep watch over the campus school. This was strongly countered by my realization that total separation was a necessity. I had just about finalized the process when my studies were interrupted by a phone call from Terry. The message he related hit me like a sledgehammer - Bill had taken his own life. The feelings of guilt associated with this reality were overwhelming. Why had we so focused on the needs of the children that we had ignored the signs of psychological stress manifested by our colleague? Was there something we could have done to reassure Bill that he was so important to all of us which might have prevented this tragedy? At Bill's wake, his fiancée assured me that there was no way any of us could have known the roots of his unhappiness or behaved any more supportively toward him. Nonetheless, my sensitivity to the psychological impact of working with children whose primary disability was that of emotional disturbance was forever heightened as a result of this sad epilogue to my years on the Hill.

Over the past twenty years, I have frequently returned to Hillside to visit and observe the progress the school has made. For three years prior to moving to Florida, Jackie served as its highly successful Director of Education. Today it is one of the finest programs of its kind in the Northeast.

Participating on a regular basis with children who are fighting valiantly to preserve their sanity and make something of their lives can be the most inspiring experience a special educator can have. Those of us who have been fortunate to be a part of this aspect of our profession frequently leave our heart in residential treatment facilities. As John Cameron Swayzee might suggest, "It takes a lickin', but keeps on tickin'." Maybe, someday again before my career is over, another opportunity to serve in such a setting might come my way.

Little Bit Country,
Little Bit Rock and Roll

*T*he 1972-73 academic year was one which offered the opportunity to reflect upon the field of special education in a thoughtful and challenging environment. Syracuse University, one of our nation's finest academic institutions, had offered me a graduate assistantship to study special education administration under Dr. Dan Sage, a leading figure in our profession. The chance to develop a higher level of expertise which would hopefully enhance my future employability was too lucrative to pass up. In addition, with the federal government picking up the tab, there was no doubt that the price was right.

Living with our three young children (ages six, four, and two) in a two bedroom apartment in married-student housing, the year went ever so slowly. Frequently making contact with Dr. Blatt on campus, however, helped to provide the motivation to fuel the engine of a future change agent. Fantasizing about what it would be like to hold down a major leadership position in special education, we dutifully carried out the rights of passage associated with graduate study on a full-time basis. Visits to local, state, and federal leaders to observe them conducting their regular professional activities only served to accelerate our interest in finding the next employment opportunity on the ladder to success.

Upon successful completion of the university school year, I was employed by the local Association for Retarded Children on a temporary basis while I eagerly waited for my ship to come in. While the administrative role I played there was transitional in nature, it did provide me with the opportunity to learn about two new areas of special education, -pre-school and adult services. The twelve weeks that I spent at the ARC were instrumental in developing my interest in such programs which would ultimately be areas of exploration in my next professional endeavor.

In mid-July, it became evident that I needed to become more proactive in seeking full-time employment for the fall, if support of my family was to continue to be an attainable goal. At the time, it had come to my attention that one of the few unfilled leadership positions in New York State was the job of Director of Special Education at the Cayuga County Board of Cooperative Educational Services (BOCES). Receiving little recognition from a letter of inquiry I'd sent about the position, it became necessary to explore alternative methods of getting my foot in the door of this organization, which I discovered was located somewhere between Rochester and Syracuse in the Finger Lakes Region.

One afternoon after work, Tom Goodman, a professional colleague, and I were consuming liquid refreshment in an effort to beat the heat. I mentioned the difficulty I had encountered in becoming recognized as a potential administrator in Cayuga County. "I think I have a friend who works for that agency. Let me give him a call and see if I can get you an interview," Tom volunteered. Three days later I was sitting in the office of the District Superintendent discussing a variety of issues related to my potential for serving effectively within his organization. It was obvious from the outset that he and I shared a lot in common, but I was more than a little bit concerned that it had taken almost a full year to fill this vacant position. At the conclusion of our discussion, he asked me to return a week later to be interviewed by their "screening committee."

That weekend I drove throughout the region served by the BOCES in order to ascertain the nature and educational needs of the varied communities served by this organization. Talking to local people, looking at school facilities, and perusing the newspaper gave me a good grasp of the area's value system relative to public education. As I sat down to meet with the screening committee, I quickly became thankful that I had made the weekend sojourn.

Chaired by the District Superintendent of the BOCES, the committee included a school psychologist employed by BOCES, a building principal from a small city school district, and the chief school administrator from a rural school district. Their questions were direct and probing, but asked in such a manner as to convey trust and honesty. By relating my answers in such a manner to include what I had learned about their respective communities, we quickly developed a rapport during the interview process putting everyone at ease. It was clear that the District Superintendent would make the ultimate decision but the relationship that existed between myself and the group made for a most enjoyable two hours. As I left, the District Superintendent informed me that I would hear from him in a few days.

After a forty minute drive back to my office at the ARC, I was greeted by the switchboard operator who informed me I had a call holding. Picking up the phone, I instantaneously recognized the voice on the other end of the line.

"The committee made me promise I wouldn't let you get away. When can you start as our Director of Special Education?" I knew immediately that my life and career had just turned dramatically in the right direction.

The concept of Boards of Cooperative Educational Services (BOCES) dates back to 1949 when creative educators at the state level decided it might be a good idea for small school districts throughout the state to pool their resources in a cost-effective manner in order to provide certain unique services for their localities. Over time vocational education, special education, and media centers became the primary service systems provided through the more than forty BOCES across the state of New York. Many other states also embraced this concept of intermediate units and it is now fairly common to see such service models being utilized by smaller school districts.

The ironic aspect of my accepting employment with a BOCES was certainly not lost on me, as I signed my first letter of agreement with the agency. During the 1966-67 school year while teaching in suburban Rochester, I led the opposition against the BOCES take over of special education classes in the region. Motivated purely by fiscal incentives inherent with BOCES participation, school superintendents in the vicinity were about to turn over their district operated programs to the leadership of this unproven governmental entity. Seventeen teachers, acutely aware of the high quality of existing services, protested this take over and challenged the feasibility of such a decision relative to the best interests of children. Meetings held with local BOCES officials only exacerbated the level of distrust among the effected special educators. Little could be done to dissuade cost-conscious administrators from this major programmatic change. Not accepting of the manner in which this change took place, I turned down a BOCES offer to continue teaching my same class under their supervision and joined the staff of a contiguous school district which had decided to operate their own special education program. It proved to be a wise decision at the time, and seven years later the bitterness of that experience had long worn off.

The Cayuga County BOCES was one of the smaller such intermediate units in the state and, as such, struggled for both resources and recognition. Of its seven component school districts, six were rural and the seventh was a small city of 35,000 inhabitants. Long and narrow, the county was bordered by Lake Ontario on the north and two Finger Lakes on the east and west. The city of Auburn was the center of the region and the economic hub around which most activities revolved. Syracuse was thirty miles to the east and Rochester sixty five miles to the west, if one craved a significantly higher level of excitement. Directly south was the city of Ithaca, where scenic beauty and college students were plentiful.

The BOCES campus, just south of the city of Auburn, contained a small vocational training center and a temporary office complex. Cultivating a cost-effective image, the BOCES leadership left no doubt in the taxpayers mind that thrift was a high priority. All except one of the agency's special education programs in 1973 were conducted in classrooms rented by BOCES in local school buildings. Unlike the vast majority of intermediate units, the Cayuga County BOCES had not constructed a special education center for the purpose of housing programs for children with disabilities. A wise decision, years ahead of its time, this singular factor had a critical impact on how these seven communities dealt with their exceptional children and what role the BOCES Director of Special Education played in providing meaningful services.

The Auburn Enlarged School District represented nearly forty percent of the region's student population. The three small districts to the north and the three similar districts to the south each supplied about ten percent of the student pool served by the agency. All seven districts held high expectations for themselves and the BOCES that served their individual needs. The chief school officers from these districts met regularly with the BOCES District Superintendent, and both the levels of cooperation and communication were high. The BOCES Board of Education was made up of representatives from local component boards of education meeting monthly to set policy and direction for the agency.

It was obvious from the outset that the Cayuga BOCES was a vibrant organization made up of hard driving individuals who took intense pride in the quality of services they could provide for their districts. While occupational and special education were their largest programs numerically, significant efforts were being mounted in such areas as labor relations, planning, instructional support services, and adult education. Each of these services was led by a director or coordinator who reported directly to the District Superintendent. This unusually flat organizational structure maximized the opportunity for clear communication with the Chief Executive Officer, and allowed his high level of energy and expectations to permeate the organization. It was readily apparent that if one was to be successful in the agency, he or she would have to adjust quickly to the benefits of such an organizational structure without falling into some of the potential pitfalls. As August of 1973 found me settling into my new office, I couldn't wait to try out my newly-honed skills in this challenging environment.

Having spent the first ten years of my professional career working in urban and suburban settings, and having grown up in a large city environment, adjusting to the conditions of rural public education would take some effort. On one of my first days on the job, the superintendent had arranged for one of my school psychologists to take me on a tour of the county's southern end. Riding throughout the countryside between the various schools we visited, he was careful to point out how poor some of our students' living conditions were. The schools we visited were well kept, obviously the hub of most community activity. The principals and clerical staff I met all seemed very friendly and anxious to work toward our common objectives.

Returning to the office that afternoon, I hurried into the superintendent's office to inform him of the benefit derived from my tour. Filled with enthusiasm after meeting so many of my new colleagues, I blurted out, "Paul, I met the Board of Education President from one of the districts and he's a farmer."

"Not only that, he's also a millionaire," replied my new boss. He was well aware that I sure had a lot to learn about country living. Overly focused on the poverty image that was being created by my tour guide, I hadn't realized that some of those larger farms we had been passing were highly profitable for those who owned them. So much for the city slicker.

Soon thereafter, at a meeting of the BOCES Board of Education, I was provided with another lesson demonstrative of the local citizenry's unique skills. As the meeting went along, I noticed a rather large but agile fly buzzing around the room. Somewhat annoyed by its pesky presence, I was pleasantly thrilled to observe one of our rural board members calmly reach his hand up ever so slowly and grasp the fly while in full flight. I started to applaud, unaware that hardly anyone else in the room had observed this unique feat. My applause drew the quizzical looks of many of those in attendance. This must be a skill we didn't master growing up on city playgrounds, I thought to myself as the meeting continued.

I attempted to meet as many of the key personnel from the seven component school districts as possible before the school year began. It became rather clear that within each of these small communities everyone knew almost everyone else. If you were interviewing someone for a teacher aide position, they would mention the names of two or three people who I should somehow have known. It suddenly became very evident that one must be careful what one says in front of whom because it was only a matter of hours before the entire community heard about it. In addition, it quickly became apparent that I needed to tone down some of the university level jargon that was so fashionable just weeks before. Sending out a memo to school principals and wishing to portray myself as fairly articulate, I had included an N.B. (Latin for note well) at the end of the memo. Two days later, one of my psychologists called to inform me that the memo had caused much confusion for his elementary principal. It seems that the principal had called him to express his concern that while he realized that L.D. kids had Learning Disabilities and E.D. kids were Emotionally Disturbed, who the hell were N.B. students?

As the school year began and I had the opportunity to visit all of my classes, the nature and needs of the children we served became more apparent. Many of those we served were so designated as a result of cultural, familial retardation. Their families had produced generations of slow learning children and the professionals working in the schools could trace the family tree to explain just why the current student had the learning and/or behavioral problems he or she had. While it seemed a rather self-fulfilling life cycle and potentially unfair for the children, it did allow for improved social service and special education support for families in need. Seeing for the first time children from rural poverty, I was struck by the impact of that condition. Where the urban poor at least had some awareness of agencies that could provide some level of support, their rural counterparts appeared devastated by the hopelessness of their situation. The eyes of these children vividly depicted the depth of their need for nurturing, both physically and psychologically. The ability of our society to respond effectively to this challenge is one of the greatest tests of our system of government.

Critical to the success as a middle manager is the knowledge that your superordinate is highly respected and willingly supportive of the values you are attempting to promulgate. Fortunately, as I assumed my role at the Cayuga County BOCES, this factor was certainly in place. Paul Haley, District Superintendent of the BOCES, led our organization in such a manner as to instill in his administrators a strong willingness to take the risks necessary to achieve excellence. Known as "Haley's Comets," his middle managers were young, outspoken, and appropriately abrasive when it came to advocating for the values that would serve the best interests of the children and school districts making up this intermediate unit. His incredible strength of character, quick wit, and ability to relate to people of various backgrounds provided a level of support for our organization that was critical to our overall success. An Irish Catholic athlete who had grown up in Western New York, he quickly became the epitome of the big brother I never had. Knowing he was always there in support of the ideals I was attempting to instill within the system gave me the confidence to be proactive in creating new services for exceptional children.

Given my career template up to this point in time, it was hard to believe I was embarking upon a commitment of effort that would last for eleven years. Knowledgeable that most school administrators moved approximately every three years, I was determined to find the ideal environment in which to raise my family and stay there as long as possible. Fortunately, my new position offered me the unique opportunity to facilitate such a strategy.

Seven miles east of Cayuga County was the village of Skaneateles, New York. Having driven through this bucolic community at the northern end of a beautiful lake on a number of occasions, I always marveled at what a perfect venue it would be to raise a family. When presented with the opportunity to make this dream come true, I quickly purchased a residence on the main street that would ultimately insure that my children would be able to maximize the enjoyment of their childhood. Great job, super boss, and ideal place to live and raise my family - I sure couldn't ask for much more.

Early that fall at a meeting of the school psychologists from our various school districts, I inquired as to whether or not there were any disabled children in the county who were not receiving the special education services they needed. In response, I was informed by the psychologist who had been on my selection committee that in fact there was a fifteen year old girl in his district who was unserved. Living in a mobile home with her parents, she was both mentally retarded and severely emotionally disturbed. State and local agencies dedicated to serving either the mentally retarded or the emotionally disturbed had refused all involvement with this young lady. Naive, but determined, I suggested that her mother come to my office prior to my going on a home visit.

At first her mother presented herself as a caring but frustrated parent who along with her daughter had been victims of an insensitive bureaucratic system. Recanting a series of program rejections, she painted a picture of unfair professionals whose level of incompetence resulted in her child having to sit home rather than grow and learn like other children. When given the opportunity, I interjected what I thought was a relevant question, "Tell me, how do you deal with your daughter when she begins her aggressive physical outbursts?"

"Oh, we use one of those things the farmers use when they want to get the cattle moving. It works quite well with her," she said.

It was mid-morning of the next day before I realized she was talking about an electric cattle prod. Racing into the superintendents office, I proposed we go into Family Court to force the State of New York to develop services for children who combine mental retardation with emotional disturbance as dual handicapping conditions. Despite his being a state employee, he agreed we should take such legal action.

A month later, both the state Commissioner of Education and Commissioner of Mental Hygiene forfeited, and the judge ordered that I be given the power and fiscal resources to create a program for this young girl. Removing her from her inappropriate home environment, I combined the services of the state Office of Mental Retardation with psychiatric services from the state Psychiatric Center supporting the school program operating under the BOCES jurisdiction. Starting out with only this one student, it ultimately grew to serve others with similar needs in the Central New York region. While psychiatrists may never accept the value of counseling the mentally retarded, if this is the only way we can prevent the use of cattle prods as an alternative measure, such treatment will continue to take place.

It soon became evident to me that there were certain sociological realities challenging educators who work in sparsely populated areas. Graduates of the local school system who performed well in school many times went on to college and never returned home again, except to visit family. There was (other than teaching) little in the way of employment opportunities in these small communities. As a result, over time, a large share of the taxpayer base for the school district was made up of adults who had not fared very well when they were in school. Their lack of support for the values and goals of the school, therefore, were many times passed on to their children or were reflected in their behavior when the school staff looked for assistance. For example, parents who had been disciplined as children "out behind the woodshed" couldn't quite understand the child abuse legislation passed in the early 1970s which required reporting by school officials of suspicion of such practices. Ultimately, the gap between middle class educators and rural poor constituents needed careful attention, skillful communications, and frequent negotiation.

Recognizing that the fiscal resources at the local level were extremely limited, it became incumbent upon the special education administrator to seek out alternative funding sources. Three major methods for overcoming this hurdle quickly came to mind:

1. Changing the state funding formula for special education students.

2. Developing opportunities for interagency cooperation so as to pool existing resources.

3. Improving my skills at grant writing to take advantage of federal, state, and private funding sources.

Considerable time and effort were spent in the early 1970s by advocates for exceptional children across New York State with the intention of increasing state-level fiscal commitment to special education programs. Prior to that time, the funding formula had been woefully inadequate and lacking in the ability to insure that money intended for special education would actually be spent by school districts for that purpose. New changes in the state-aid formula were forthcoming, causing administrators and school boards to view special educational services as less burdensome for local tax bases.

In sparsely populated areas with limited economic development, agencies serving the disabled, in both the public and private sectors, found themselves scrambling for the resources necessary to serve their chosen clientele. Other then regional support services from the large state agencies,

Cayuga County was limited in the number of service providers for disabled children and adults. Fortunately, however, the two major private agencies were vibrant and dedicated in serving the needs of their constituents. Both the local chapters of the Association for Retarded Children and the United Cerebral Palsy were dynamic organizations which combined parent driven boards of directors with professional staffs eager to provide quality services.

After a short period of getting to know each other, their respective Executive Directors and I developed a working relationship. This relationship was sensitive to the reality that, if we were going to be able to develop high quality service delivery systems, sharing of resources would be essential. With this in mind, I worked with the State Education Department to secure funds to staff a pre-school program which was immediately located at the U.C.P. facility. In this way we could take advantage of the therapeutic services they could provide for our children and their families. In addition, U.C.P. staff began providing physical and occupational therapy in the public schools for children who needed this service, paid for under third party payments. Working with the ARC staff, we were able to initiate an adult vocational training program utilizing occupational education funds supplied through a grant from the State Education Department. By behaving in this manner, we were jointly able to demonstrate to both state and local funding sources that our model of interagency cooperation resulted in making their investment go much farther to serve the handicapped than in other parts of New York State. In addition, the spirit of such cooperation set a tone throughout the respective agencies and the community at large which resulted in continuous support for each of our organizations.

The ability to tap into these available funding sources was a direct result of my having the good fortune of working at BOCES with the finest grantsman in New York State. Stu Naidich brought new meaning to the word indefatigable. He was driven by the beauty of the written word and its ability to acquire the much needed fiscal resources to facilitate change in rural school districts. He inspired all of us to stay up all night writing quality proposals for review by funding sources. As we supplied program concepts and the current jargon, Stu would verbally package these ideas in such a manner so as to enhance their chances of being funded. His record of successful grant proposals was unmatched, and the impact his work had on the children of Cayuga County is immeasurable. His ability to make our program dreams come true created an aura of hope that permeated the schools throughout the county and inspired his colleagues to challenge their creativity with each new cycle of requests for proposals. The comprehensive service system which was created for exceptional children in the region owed much of its initiation to the pen of this determined and articulate educational leader.

When one reflects upon a special educator's career lasting the past three decades, it is readily apparent that a considerable portion of this time was spent changing people's attitudes about those who are different. Whether urban, suburban, or rural populations, there is little difference in the level of appreciation for the human potential of exceptional individuals. While rarely by design, our society has nonetheless failed to expose itself to opportunities for learning more about children with disabilities.

Cayuga County BOCES had, for some time prior to my arrival, operated a program for children categorized as trainable mentally retarded which had received well deserved kudos for its hard working and competent staff. Based on principles of open education and family grouping, considerable time was spent providing these children (with I.Q.s between twenty and fifty) with the opportunity to function in the community at large. As a result of these normalized learning activities, the students' social skills developed impressively, and they were a most gregarious group of youngsters to work with. We felt very happy that the community members at large had grown to accept and understand our students during the process of enriching their instructional program.

One summer afternoon, I sat down with two key staff-members from the T.M.R. program in a popular restaurant in downtown Auburn. As we ordered our meal, a large group of customers began to congregate around two large tables situated next to us. The customers, carrying presents and in a jovial mood, indicated that a celebration was about to take place. As they assembled, we recognized a teenage girl with them who was from our BOCES T.M.R. program. Upon seeing two of her teachers, the girl waved happily. Once seated around the two tables, the group signaled to the waitress they were ready to order. The waitress moved purposefully around the tables until she arrived at the young lady with obvious mental retardation. Stopping abruptly, she turned to the adult women sitting next to the girl, and in a voice loud enough for us to hear, inquired, "Does she eat?" Momentarily stunned by this well-intended question, we quickly realized our job of educating the community was far from complete.

Realizing that attracting enthusiastic, well-trained teachers into a sparsely populated area in the years ahead might be a real challenge, I embarked upon a plan to help local people gain state certification in teaching special education. Once again, drawing upon the spirit of interagency cooperation, we worked with the ARC and two colleges to create a high quality teacher training program running each summer. The ARC operated a day camp on the shore of Owasco Lake which provided full recreational services for the county's children with mental retardation. Local school districts generously provided bussing to and from this beautiful setting for those enrolled. Arranging with colleges which trained special educators to offer course work at the camp for interested students, we were able to provide local young adults the opportunity to pursue certification in an environment where they could gain experience working with exceptional children. The children, the teacher trainees, the

ARC, the colleges, and ultimately BOCES, all reaped the benefits of this unique endeavor. A few years later we expanded our relationship with the colleges so that we were able to offer our provisionally certified staff graduate level courses taught on the BOCES campus leading to a master's degree in special education.

Among the many built-in advantages of working in an intermediate unit like BOCES was the proximity to vocational training options for high school-aged children. In the mid 1970s, however, access to such training options for disabled students across our state was limited. Fortunately, just prior to my employment with BOCES, they created a program geared toward providing such learning experience for special education students. Once again, utilizing grant monies administered by the State Education Department, staff were hired who were interested in teaching occupational skills to students categorized as mentally retarded, learning disabled, or emotionally disturbed. The program mode that we developed allowed students to explore a variety of vocational options before specializing in-depth in one occupational area. The key to the program's success was our insistence that the special education teacher and the vocational teacher communicate regularly on individual student progress or problems. In order to provide access for our higher functioning pupils with disabilities into regular occupational courses, we eventually created a resource teacher model in our vocational center. The resource teacher would move throughout the center to support the special education students in those areas of the occupational education curriculum where they required extra assistance.

Sensitive to the importance of building sound working relationships between special and occupational educators the State Education Department initiated a series of weekend training activities for members of these respective faculties. Greater understanding of disabilities, and increased mutual respect for each other's role in providing a total program for secondary level students resulted from these high quality staff development activities. I was fortunate to be invited to participate as a trainer at many of these sessions, and I developed a much more significant respect for the challenges faced by my colleagues in vocational education.

Soon after the start of my first year at BOCES, we held an open house for parents of children who were served in our popular T.M.R. program. A bright, enthusiastic, and dedicated staff had developed a wonderful working relationship with these parents, so they came out in large numbers to meet the newly appointed Director of Special Education. Meeting each of them individually upon their arrival, I was pleased with the positive attitude they had about their child's special education program. My speech would be short and geared toward reassuring them of my interest in maintaining this high level of service for our students. Upon completing my message, I proceeded to ask if there were any questions.

"Tell me Mr. Costello," inquired a rather tall father with a cynical tone of voice. "How long will you be here until you move to Albany to work for the State Education Department?"

Initially stunned by his implication, it dawned on me that the last two incumbents in my position had spent less than two years each in this position before moving on to the state capital. These parents, therefore, harbored a concern about the commitment I would have to their children.

"It is my intention to serve this BOCES for a good long time and during that period my goal will be to insure that each of your offspring will thoroughly enjoy his or her childhood." Little did I realize that all of their children would graduate from the program before I would move on. Ironically, the father who asked that question became a school board member in one of our component districts and was one of our biggest supporters.

In the spring of 1974, I received a call one afternoon from a staff member of the state education department. Actually it was one of my predecessors - the person who had only stayed in the job three months. He explained to me that they had just discovered regulatory language on the books that referred to something called a "Committee on the Handicapped." The problem was that nobody in Albany had any idea what this committee was or how it should function in order to carry out its apparently undefined duties. He inquired if I would be willing to host a day long gathering of key individuals in the field of special education from all over the state in order to see if we could determine the purpose and role of the Committee on the Handicapped (C.O.H.). Inquisitive by nature, I quickly agreed to facilitate this group process, and one of my school psychologists agreed to develop a position paper for department publication based on the outcome of the meeting.

Held at a motel adjacent to the Syracuse Airport, this meeting drew over thirty eager participants, reflecting the perspective of parents, teachers, administrators, professors, and bureaucrats. We had no trouble whatsoever in getting people to express their opinions on how this committee should involve itself in relation to special education. By day's end, everyone was exhausted as they boarded their planes for the return flight home, optimistic that our work would lead to a much needed reform relative to how children become eligible for special education services.

To his great credit, David Petras, my school psychologist, was able to create a meaningful document for review by the State Education Department, as a result of the significant amount of input given by the participants at the conference. Committee membership, due process issues, referral procedures, and evaluation criteria were spelled out in such a manner as to clearly define the responsibilities of the newly created C.O.H. In addition, we included a section in the paper describing the role of the C.O.H. as a "child advocate" for children with disabilities. Extremely well written, and strongly supportive of the rights of children, this section drew the only negative reaction from the reviewers at the state level, who suggested that we change the term "child advocacy" to "mild advocacy." Our response to this request was that we strongly felt it was an oxymoron (with the emphasis on the moron) to use such a term as "mild advocacy." Two years later, when the new state legislation dealing with the education of children with handicapping conditions became law, the Committee on the Handicapped was the cornerstone of the entire process of serving exceptional children.

As it became more and more apparent that massive change in the special education system was on the horizon, the need for public school personnel to become prepared to deal effectively with exceptional children mounted. Key players within the change process would most certainly be the school principals serving the over seven hundred public school districts in New York State. Unless they felt comfortable dealing on a day-to-day basis with the issues created by serving children with disabilities in their schools, positive program outcomes would be difficult to achieve. Attuned to this critical need, I eagerly joined with friends and colleagues at the state department level to develop a training instrument which would ultimately be utilized from one end of our state to the other over a three year period.

Based on the concept of simulation, this training module provided participants the opportunity to experience the kind of day-to-day challenges that would occur when special education programs were located in their individual schools. School board meetings, parent confrontations, irate phone calls, memos from the superintendent, and teacher conferences took place during the three days of training. Principals were able to share with their peers just how they would deal effectively with the issues presented. An extremely popular training model, these workshops provided those who conducted them with the opportunity to better understand the behavior of those who would see to it that the promise of the new legislation would become reality. Starting at Niagara Falls, we gradually worked across the state over the three years until we reached the tip of Long Island. It was fascinating to see how over four hundred educational leaders dealt with the same issues, many of which were emotional in nature. They learned as much from each other as they did from us.

One of the toughest challenges in the workshop required the participants to develop a meaningful I.E.P. for a young girl, who although very bright, suffered from severe cerebral palsy. In mostly all cases, the principals found a way to provide her with educational services in their buildings with her non-disabled peers. On Long Island, however, the group decided almost unanimously to ship her off to a segregated day school for physically disabled children. The next day, as we were showing a film strip illustrating a point we were trying to make, one of the participants jumped up, pointing to the screen and said, "That's my nephew!"

When we turned the lights back on he arose once again and addressed the group.

"You know how you people were unwilling to serve that little girl in your schools yesterday? Let me tell you about my nephew. He has cerebral palsy too and thank God his school principal worked with us to put in ramps and adjust desks so that he could go to school with his friends. Last year he finished his Master's Degree and is now earning over $25,000 a year. I developed a mechanical fishing pole for him to use and he has caught some big fish not far from here. I sure hope you people take the time to re-think your position on the capability of children with this condition."

As we smiled to ourselves, he sat down and the stunned group of principals had learned something we had always known - the beauty of this kind of training is that it's not the trainers who do the most significant teaching. While these workshops required my being away from home for numerous weekends, the potential for impacting positively on thousands of children with disabilities, and the opportunity to observe the development of supportive attitudes towards special education in mainstream settings was more than enough of a reward.

During my third year at BOCES, the high and low points of human experience came to visit. At the mid-winter meeting of the District Superintendents, honors were bestowed on various BOCES educational programs or services from around New York State. In the field of special education there were three programs selected for such recognition. The administration and staff of each program were invited to present their accomplishments before an audience of the leading educators from our state. The Commissioner of Education addressed the dinner guests who gathered to pay tribute to these fine educational efforts. The Cayuga County BOCES T.M.R. program and the Interagency Pre-School program were two of the three special education services selected for this meaningful recognition. Paul Haley, myself, and some of our dedicated staff enjoyed a wonderful and proud trip to Albany, in order to demonstrate to those assembled leaders the results of our determined efforts on behalf of exceptional children. The thrill of the experience was tempered only by the realization that my mother was lying in a nursing home in Rochester, suffering from terminal stomach cancer, and my father was sitting home alone, nursing an irreparably broken heart. The next few months were the worst of my life . However, my mother's example of the impact of determined compassion for those of our fellow human beings in need would last in my memory forever. Hopefully, knowing of the recognition we received, and that alternatives to what she had viewed in **Christmas In Purgatory** were now in place, allowed her to rest more peacefully.

After three years in a position such as mine, the BOCES Board of Education needed to decide whether or not to grant me tenure. Should they decide not to, I was out of a job. If they decided to retain my services, it would be legally next to impossible to ever sever our employment relationship. Paul Haley assured me that with his recommendation, my tenure was sure to pass. Having never seen the board go against his wishes, I had no reason to doubt him.

As the day of the board meeting approached, I submitted to our Associate Superintendent a bid on one of our fleet cars that was being sold to the highest bidder, in accordance with state law. An ugly green Plymouth with eighty thousand hard miles on the odometer, BOCES did not expect to receive many bids from the public who looked it over carefully. Nonetheless, I was quite surprised to learn that my bid of a mere two hundred dollars made me its new owner. The only problem was that the Board of Education had to vote on both my tenure and the acceptance of my bid at the same meeting.

Not wanting to take unnecessary risks, I asked the Superintendent to arrange the agenda for the board meeting in such a manner that they voted me tenure prior to learning about the bid awards. Thus protected from appearing to be a skinflint, both measures passed unanimously. Job security and a new car (which would last for over three years) - not a bad night's work.

As special educators, school officials, and parents began interacting with each other more intensively as required under the new Federal and State statutes, changes in public policy relating to the education of children with disabilities were commonplace. Under the auspices of Chapter 853, the Commissioner's Advisory Panel was established to advise the commissioner of needed changes related to special education. As past-president of the New York State Association of Special Education Administrators, I was asked to be a member of that prestigious panel. Thrilled to be nominated, I happily served a three year term, along with twenty-four others, representing parents, teachers, educational leaders, professional organizations, and individuals with disabilities. Having been involved in the creation of the C.A.P., it was gratifying to participate in public policy recommendations with such a fine group of people. While individual members brought varied perspectives to the table and debate was frequently heated, a common bond existed within the group that always seemed to protect the best interests of children. A unique kinship developed between panel members who had very little in common. Each of us walked away from these meetings with a greater appreciation for how public policy evolves in our complex democratic society.

The stark reality of working with exceptional children in rural America was never far from my level of consciousness. One day in mid-January of 1976, I received a call from a woman whose name I did not recognize.

"I called," she said, "to let you know that Dan can come to school now."

"I'm sorry," I replied, "I don't understand what you mean by that."

"Well, when he was five, I registered Dan for school back in Pennsylvania, and they told me he could not attend until he was toilet trained. He's toilet trained now, can I send him to your school?"

"Well, I'm glad you called," I said. "We don't have any such restrictions in this state, so let's get Dan in here. By the way, how old is your youngster now?"

"Dan just turned seventeen," she replied.

Dumbstruck, I realized that this unfortunate woman had spent the past twelve years attempting to toilet train her son who had severe retardation so that he might attend school for the first time. Despite federal, state, and local child-find efforts, the two of them were totally unaware of Dan's right to an appropriate education. After meeting him the next day, I was devastated by how such prolonged absence from services had affected this young man's life. With his bad heart and other health problems, it would be extremely difficult, in the next four years, to make up for all the lost time; but we would sure give it one hell of a good try.

On the other extreme, at about the same time, we created, for the first time, an infant stimulation program which employed a special education teacher to work with children birth to three. A downward extension of our pre-school offering, this service provided parents of young infants with support in their own homes in the care and early education of children with handicapping conditions.

One day as I sat in my office discussing with this teacher her unique new role, she explained in great depth her newest referral. It seemed a local pediatrician suggested that she begin serving a child with multiple handicaps who was still being cared for in the maternity ward of our local hospital. Upon accepting this exciting challenge, she soon learned her first required activity would be to go to the hospital and learn how to feed the child intravenously. She would then train his mother to carry out this procedure at home. With awesome suddenness, it dawned on me the extent to which special educators had committed themselves in the service of exceptional children. As strictly an education agency, my department, through our interagency cooperation program, was serving disabled individuals from birth to age sixty. For a mostly rural, lower socioeconomic region to be able to provide such a high quality, lifelong continuum of services was most gratifying. We soon observed that parents of children with disabilities, and state agencies faced with the decree to deinstitutionalize their clients, began moving into the county in order to receive our services.

In order to convince Congress of the need to enact PL 94-142, advocates for exceptional children testified that there were literally millions of unserved children with disabilities throughout the nation. Upon passage of the law, it then became incumbent upon local, state, and federal education officials to scour the countryside in search of these new recipients of legislative support. Each state embarked upon Child Find activities, utilizing the mass media in an attempt to identify the whereabouts of these numerous children. Always wishing to be in the forefront, New York eagerly conducted a wide range of efforts aimed at accomplishing this end.

Because of my involvement with the legislative

process, I received a phone call one day asking me if I would take part in a live television show highlighting the Child Find efforts in Central New York. Emanating from Syracuse and telecast over the Public Television Network, the format allowed for viewers to call in their questions to a panel of experts, of which I was one. I was relieved to find out that the host of the program was an old college buddy I hadn't seen in many years. I was nonetheless anxious because the calls would not be screened, and the BOCES Board of Education would be temporarily recessing their monthly meeting so that they could watch the show together in their Board Room.

After a brief, but informative overview of the Child Find's goals, our host began piping in the calls, not unlike Phil Donahue. The first few calls went rather routinely, but then I heard my old college chum announce "the next caller wants to talk about the Cayuga BOCES. Hey Mark, this call's for you."

"I would just like to say,'Thank God for the people at the Cayuga BOCES,'" said a woman caller as I began to exhale." "We took our son all over this area, and their program was the only one who would welcome him when he wasn't toilet trained. We sure appreciate the fine work they are doing with the children."

While I am sure our Board of Education and the District Superintendent were proud of the public kudos, I couldn't help but think that after fifteen years in the field of public education, it was interesting the things I would be remembered for.

Our teacher aides were a most hardworking and dedicated group of individuals whose entire focus was upon the best interests of the children they served. Unfortunately, the BOCES salary scale barely surpassed the federal minimum wage and there was very little future for someone who toiled with such a high degree of commitment. Morale within the group was unusually high, and we made every attempt to award them in other than monetary ways for their critical contributions to the program's success.

One incident, totally unanticipated, seriously undermined my efforts at making these fine people feel good about themselves. Our T.M.R. students who had been successfully participating in our vocational programs, were now ready to experience the work-study phase of their training. Upon successful completion, a select few were gradually eased into carefully selected competitive jobs. Two of our students, appreciative of all the support and training they received from the BOCES staff, came to visit after they had been working for a short period of time. During the visit both students and staff radiated with well-deserved pride.

About ten minutes into the visit, one of my teacher aides approached me with a most interesting question. "Mark, I noticed from Louie's pay check that he's making twenty cents an hour more than I am, and I've been with BOCES for five years. Can we do anything about that?"

I'm sure my answer was of little comfort, but my appreciation for the contributions of these dedicated people will continue to grow, as the accomplishments of those they served bear testimony to the effectiveness of their efforts.

Soon thereafter, I was contacted by a colleague in the far northern most region of New York State who asked me if I would be willing to drive up there to conduct a one day training workshop for his teacher aides. Aware of how appreciative people from that remote area are of efforts people make on their behalf, I was glad to oblige. Arising early in the morning, I drove three and a half hours to a small community located on the St. Lawrence River where a BOCES vocational center was located. Entering this clean, well-kept building, I was about to have the most unusual experience of my life.

As I walked into the large area where a group of thirty women were seated, it became obvious by the equipment in the rooms that it was a nursing education suite. Never having been involved in staff development activities in the past, my audience appeared somewhat nervous. What was about to happen certainly wouldn't lessen their degree of anxiety.

Walking across the front of the room on my way to the instructor's desk, I passed in front of a tall double locker. As I laid my briefcase on the desk, I looked out at the assembled group.

"Good morning ladies. I just drove up here from Skaneateles and am very impressed by your nice vocational center. I think we're all going to have a good time today discussing children with disabilities. Before we start, though, please bear with me for a moment. When I walked past that locker over there, I had the strangest feeling that someone was inside it. I think we'll all feel better after I check it out."

At this point, the group rustled in their seats as I began to walk toward the locker. I could imagine their disappointment in realizing their first workshop was being conducted by a lunatic. Quickly opening the double doors to the locker, we were all confronted by a five foot human skeleton. The participants let out a collective scream you could hear all the way to Canada, and I nearly suffered a heart attack. To this day, I still don't know why I did what I did, but it sure provided me with a high level of audience attention for the next six hours.

While membership within the various intermediate educational units (BOCES) throughout New York State remains rather constant, there is a complicated process through which school districts may switch from one such agency to another. While rarely taken advantage of, this procedure was utilized twice during my eleven years with the Cayuga BOCES. The Skaneateles School District, where my three children attended classes, decided to request, from the State Education Department, permission to leave the Onondaga-Madison counties BOCES (of which they had long been members) in order to become a member of our BOCES. After a careful study by the S.E.D. of the value of such a move to all three groups involved, this highly political

122

process culminated in Skaneateles becoming one of our component school districts. As a result of this acquisition, the name of our organization was changed to reflect that our new member was located in Onondaga County. We then officially became the Cayuga-Onondaga BOCES with eight component school districts.

A few years later the Jordan-Elbridge School District, also from Onondaga County, made a similar request and was granted approval to become our ninth component district. Both of these districts, while partially rural in nature, were primarily bedroom communities to the city of Syracuse. Their becoming members of our organization brought significant increases in student numbers and wealth to our BOCES. These factors greatly enhanced our organization's ability to develop new and diverse service options for the years ahead. This change in membership also expanded the variety of services available to children with disabilities, the result of which continued to benefit the children we served. The linkage with suburban values and expectations helped to round out a more heterogeneous organization of small school districts, which cooperatively depend upon each other's uniqueness and creativity to solve common problems. Paul Haley's genius in pulling off this political coup will long be appreciated by those who derive the benefits of this union.

With Skaneateles now in the fold, the variety of issues I was called upon to deal with became more diverse. At the request of a colleague, I walked down to the village one evening to meet with the local president of the Women of Rotary. Sitting in her living room overlooking the lake, she explained to me her group's interest in creating a college scholarship fund to support young people with disabilities. My role would be twofold - helping them develop selection criteria and firing up the troops at their kickoff luncheon at the Skaneateles County Club so that the coffers would quickly fill up. Sitting at the head table with the President, I looked at a group of some forty elderly, well-bred and well-heeled Ladies of Rotary. My purpose was to tug at their heartstrings so that they would immediately reach for their checkbooks. I finally realized how Jerry Lewis felt each Labor Day.

After lunch, as I rose to address the group, I gazed once again at a beautiful knitted train adorning the head table which would later be auctioned off as a fund raiser.

"I would like to begin by congratulating the member or members of your group who knitted this gorgeous train. Whoever the fortunate child is who will be receiving it as a gift will be happy indeed."

"Looking at it all during lunch made me reflect upon why I entered the profession of special education and reminded me of my late mother. As a child, one of my fondest memories was of my mother sitting on my bed reading my favorite story to me before I went to sleep. I'm sure you all remember **The Little Engine That Could?** It is the story of how an under-worked little engine, determined to bring the gifts over the mountain succeeded in reaching that goal."

"Many times in the past fifteen years as I've sat assisting children with mental retardation with difficult academic tasks, I've heard my mother's voice in the background. *I think I can, I think I can, I know I can.* The happy ending of that storybook exemplifies the exhilaration of being a teacher of children with disabilities."

Following my brief talk, I showed a passage from the TV movie, "Who are the DeBolts and why do they have nineteen children?" This movie depicts the life of a wonderful couple who adopted a large group of children, most of whom are refugees and/or disabled in some way. It provided vivid, visual images of beautiful children who have been overachievers, as a result of the loving environment in which they were raised. One of the scenes in the film deals with the mother explaining to the assembled family that grandma had just that day passed away. Asking the children not to cry, she encourages each of them to relate a story they most remember about their adopted grandma. The impact of this movie on those who have seen it is powerful in how it points out the human potential in each of us. Consequently, the Women of Rotary were most generous in their contributions, and a few months later we met again to decide which of the applicants would be selected for the available scholarships.

As our vocational education resource teacher program progressed, more and more children with disabilities were able to participate in regular vocational training programs. Their resource teacher would meet regularly with the various instructors in such courses as food service, cosmetology, automotive repair, and machine shop. The resource teacher would assist the students with disabilities in learning course content and mastering the vocational skills up to the level of their capability. We soon learned that this instructional model had positive benefits for the non-disabled members of the class as well. With the passage of affirmative action legislation, local employers were looking for employees who had experience working with disabled co-workers, so as to create a work environment able to accept those new employees with disabilities. Since our local high school students had experienced this type of training at BOCES, their potential for employment with local business increased.

The most impressive example of the spirit and value of this program was exemplified by a sixteen year old young man who had been part of our T.M.R. program all of his school life. Harley was a dwarf who stood just a shade over three feet and was from a family who was well represented within our special education program. Living well below the poverty level, the family members struggled to survive against gradually mounting odds. In the face of such a depressing lifestyle, Harley displayed great courage but lacked self-confidence and rarely smiled. That was until we decided to give him the opportunity to be part of the machine shop class with the big guys his own age from the local high schools.

As soon as Harley entered the shop, and with the assistance of his resource teacher began exploring the

125

various equipment, his world and self-concept expanded greatly. Some of his classmates built him a stool to sit on, which was placed on the workbench next to the particular machine he was learning to use. While certainly far from able to master most of the technical skills involved in the curriculum, he eagerly participated in those activities within his reach. His fellow students always looked for ways to include Harley in their learning activity, and the smile on his face told all of us how much better he felt about himself. Each day when the class lined up for dismissal, Harley stood proudly at the front of the line, and when the bell rang, he led the guys out the door on their way to the buses with a look of great personal satisfaction. A year-and-a-half later Harley passed away, after falling victim to complications from his numerous health problems. We were pleased that during his all too-short time on this earth, we were fortunate to be able to give him that one opportunity to stand tall with the guys in machine shop. Many of them came to his wake to express their gratitude for all he had taught them about the meaning of courage.

The key to success for any special education program is its ability to attract quality staff who will, through their daily interaction with children, make a significant difference in their lives. Fortunately, during the 1970s, interest in careers teaching exceptional children resulted in some of this country's finest young people joining our profession. When I first entered the field, very few people teaching special education classes had been appropriately trained to perform their duties. Even worse, in many areas of the state, the special education teacher was selected because of his or her inability to succeed in a regular education classroom.

During the 1970s, there was an increased awareness of the educational needs of children with disabilities. Teacher training programs were filled with bright enthusiastic young people who had responded to John F. Kennedy's earlier call for commitment to meeting the needs of our citizens with mental retardation. This increased level of public awareness resulted in an influx into special education classrooms of talented teachers, while at the same time declining enrollments were causing cutbacks in positions for regular education teachers. For the first time in history, special education administrators had a real choice of candidates when attempting to fill a position.

I was thrilled by the quality of applicants I was seeing. We had as a profession turned an important corner and our kids for the first time had gained an advantage over their non-handicapped peers. My only problem was that I had to compete in this labor market with one of the lowest salary schedules in the state and also deal with the reality that our region did not have an abundant supply of middle class eligible bachelors. Used to fighting against difficult odds, we annually struggled to gain access to the best of each year's new crop of recently graduated special education teachers.

One of the truisms I learned over the years was that teachers always maintain an active interest in their best students. Aware of this, I made it a point to always work closely with the professors from the finest special education teacher training institutions in our state. Additionally, I taught graduate courses for some of these schools so that I could achieve colleague status where that was important. Employing many of these fine teacher trainers as consultants during the school year only solidified our bonds. It was not long before the vast majority of these teacher trainers were directing their brightest and most talented graduates my way to insure that their initial teaching experience would be successful. Also they could receive consistent feedback on their student's progress.

As a result, despite our high turnover rate, we were able to consistently attract high quality special educators into our region. Later on, when the competition became more difficult, we began searching into other states whose employment market was depressed and successfully recruited exceptional teachers into our program.

While my major legacy to Cayuga County was the quality of the people we brought into the area to work as special educators, I must admit a certain weakness as a recruiter. Due to the nature of our profession, I have always felt a responsibility to give consideration to applicants who have disabilities or who might be considered in some way different. Once I recommended, to the superintendent, a candidate who had recently been paroled from the maximum security prison located in downtown Auburn. Having met him previously at the home of the Executive Director of U.C.P., I felt safe that he would be a capable teaching assistant working in our pre-school at that facility. In order to convince my boss, who was well aware of the community's disdain for the "criminal element," I pointed out to him that if BOCES did not demonstrate by its actions, a belief in rehabilitation, we would be hypocritical and might as well close our doors. He agreed and my selection did an excellent job before moving on to a more highly paying job in the community and becoming one of the biggest supporters of both U.C.P. and BOCES.

Toward the end of my tour of duty in the Finger Lakes Region, I hired two young women to teach for me who were both visually impaired. While the impact of their level of blindness had apparently not been a factor during their undergraduate teacher preparation, both of them experienced difficulties during their employment with us. As I struggled with attempting to diagnose the reason or reasons for their problems, an interesting pattern began to emerge. It seemed that they both had a tendency to over-talk with the adults they had to work with, and, as a result, communication problems existed. Additionally, those who worked with them began to question how receptive these two bright, well-trained young teachers were to feedback from others around them who were anxious to be helpful.

After even more careful scrutiny, I came to two conclusions about how the impact of their disability was negatively affecting their potential to be successful teachers.

First, the tendency to over talk was an effort to better control their environment, but in doing so they had not mastered the listening skills necessary to build positive working relationships with other adults. Secondly, the inability to process "body language" greatly deterred their ability to detect how those they were speaking to were reacting to what they were saying. Many times they would assume that silence may have meant acceptance of their ideas, when in fact the other party had turned away or actually left the conversation. I was frustrated by my attempts to provide more meaningful support to these enthusiastic young special educators, but, in sharing my observations with them we did take some steps in the right direction.

The best feature of working in an organization such as the Cayuga-Onondaga BOCES was, that with strong leadership at the top, the negative side of risk taking was significantly minimized. With this in mind, we were relatively free to experiment with program concepts that others might hesitate to embrace. One year, we decided to house a class for children with severe mental retardation in an elementary school in Auburn. While this building had housed a variety of special education classes in the past, we were interested in seeing how this unique group of children would be accepted.

The class was made up of children whose chronological ages ranged from six to nine but whose mental ages were between eight months to a year and a half. With no expressive language and very little receptive language skills, it was a task for some of these children just to roll over or make eye contact. While the community was aware that such children were no longer being placed in large state institutions, few if any of them had ever seen or heard about the needs of youngsters with severe retardation.

Early that fall, the school hosted its annual Harvest Supper to which parents brought dishes, and the principal reviewed his agenda for the new school year. Sensitive to the curiosity about the new BOCES class, he asked the new teacher to explain to the large assembled group the nature and needs of her students. As she began to speak, a hush came over the cafeteria as these concerned adults listened to her describe each of her students. As she progressed along through her presentation, the audience became quieter. A few minutes further into her explanation of how well the children had been accepted into the overall school population, those in attendance grew even quieter. It was then that I first realized that there are degrees of silence - based on the impact of the subject at hand. Soon thereafter, many of these parents began stopping by the classroom to meet the children and some of their own non-disabled offspring began volunteering in our classroom. It was a fascinating learning experience for all of us.

Many times special educators, confronted with what always seems to be an inadequate supply of options for the appropriate placement of students, decry the lack of flexibility within the system. This child is too low functioning, this one isn't being challenged enough, and that youngster shouldn't be in my class at all. It always seems like we have a lot of students who seem to fall between the cracks. There are just too many gaps in the service system in order to provide the level of homogeneous grouping every teacher, parent, and principal desires.

Having heard these concerns expressed ad nauseam, we decided to try another way of grouping students which we referred to as "gapping." We identified some children who seemed, by their learning characteristics, to fall into the "gap" between our traditional instructional groupings. Building off of those particular students we took the higher functioning children from the next lowest group (T.M.R. range) and the lowest functioning children from the next highest group (E.M.R. range). The results were incredibly successful as the kids from the higher group were now the head of their class and those who had been under-challenged in the T.M.R. class began demonstrating their true potential.

Exciting classes for teachers in our "transitional program" changed the entire focus of our service system. Some years later the same "gapping" concept proved effective when students with severe retardation were combined with somewhat higher functioning students in local school buildings. Unfortunately, we were too busy enjoying the students' success to apply any meaningful research design in an effort to document quantitatively what our hearts and minds told us was wonderfully true.

The ultimate benefit associated with being a special educator is the increased opportunity for meaningful interaction with some of the world's most beautiful children. While grudgingly admitting many beholders may have to look more deeply to find the beauty in some of our students, there are others who are bestowed with a unique gift to share with all those with whom they come in contact. Such a young boy was Scott, whose role on this earth was to radiate joy amongst the children and adults who worked with him in our T.M.R. program at BOCES.

Scott came to us from a school district that was not a component member of our BOCES, but was located seventeen miles west of Auburn. Each day, after his fifth birthday, he would bounce off the school bus ready to unleash his ever replenishing supply of charisma on all those he interacted with in our primary level class. His smile was infectious and his sense of accomplishment inspired others (staff and students) to try harder. We were frequently approached by adults who met Scott with requests to photograph him for journal articles or textbooks. One student of film making at a nearby university, with Scott's parents' permission, did an extensive video presentation featuring Scott. His ability to draw adults and other children to him was truly magical.

Every other Friday morning, I would enter the T.M.R. program armed with the paychecks for the fifteen or so staff who worked there. Well aware that the contents of those envelopes would bring an enthusiastic response from each adult, Scott would race to my side so he could play the role of paymaster. Handing out each check proudly, he eagerly accepted the appreciation of those being remunerated. His involvement in this process only served to reinforce the reality that money was not the reason to be in this business.

The unique beauty of Scott as an exceptional child was the paradoxical reality that despite his having no meaningful expressive language skills, he was such a powerful communicator. Blessed with a higher level of receptive language skills, his enthusiasm and willingness to please were outstanding compensatory behaviors which always kept him in contact with peers and adults. He attacked life with a vigor that communicated hope and perseverance. When he was absent from school for a day, the change in the mood throughout the classroom was discernible immediately. For two years, his impact on the instructional environment made working in the primary classroom a highly sought after assignment. On those many occasions when paper pushing and bureaucratic hassling were less than gratifying, my colleagues always knew where they could find me.

Because I must have consciously forgot, I was stunned to learn that it was now time for Scott to undergo the open heart surgery his doctors had been putting off until he grew stronger. While short and compact with a well muscled little body, his heart was not well equipped to provide the supply of energy he daily expended. The date of his entry into the hospital was approaching.

Frequently, when I interview teachers who will be working with children who have physical and health related disabilities, I question them about their readiness to deal with the loss of a student. You would think that in so doing, the questioner would have been better prepared for the reality that shook our campus when we learned Scott had failed to survive his operation. The sense of loss and feeling of injustice was overwhelming, tempered only by the realization of how fortunate we all felt to have been the recipients of his all too-short presence on this earth.

Attending the funeral of a child such as Scott is an experience that has a lasting impact on anyone who must endure such a loss. Wanting to somehow have the joy that was so bountiful in his life extinguish the grief that permeated throughout the church, the mourners were confronted with a beautiful rendition by the organist of "God Loves All the Children of the World." Her voice reverberating throughout the beautiful old church as his casket proceeded down the aisle, the soloist through the words of the hymn attempted to reassure us that Scott was now in the arms of someone who would love him forever as much as we had all too briefly. His spirit lives on in the hearts and minds of many of those he so dramatically touched, and it is rare that a return trip to Central New York doesn't include reminiscences of this beautiful child.

During my eleven years of service to the Cayuga-Onondaga BOCES, Paul Haley made sure that I received as sound an education as any of our students. The advantages of working in such a unique setting were lost on me at the time but are greatly appreciated today. New York State began collective bargaining in public schools in the late 1960s, and as a result school administrators began developing skills in contract management and table negotiations. I was given the opportunity to represent the Board of Education in the bargaining process and learned a lot from the endeavor.

As mentioned earlier, grant writing was another area where I was given the chance to develop necessary skills. For four months, I served as the Acting Director of Occupational Education while serving on the selection committee to find a full-time leader to assume that role. Toward the end of my tenure with the organization, I headed a task force that created the position of Director of Instructional Support Services and chaired the selection committee for filling the position. Wearing many hats was a necessity when working in a sparsely populated area but the benefit of such a learning experience is certainly invaluable.

No matter how many roles of a professional nature that I played during that time, there are still a small group of the local citizenry that think my real employment was in a significantly different line of work. One night I was invited to go out to dinner with my entire staff from our T.M.R. program. Quickly agreeing to partake in what I was sure would be a fun filled evening, it didn't dawn on me that I would be the only male in our party. Surrounded by fifteen attractive women in their 20s and 30s, I sat at the head of the table enjoying a fine meal and jovial conversation. When one of the staff returned from a trip to the rest room, she recanted for us a conversation she had overheard at the bar on her way back. It seemed that the small group of men gathered at the bar had agreed amongst themselves that I must be a pimp.

While everyone enjoyed a good laugh at my expense, the bartender answered the phone and paged one of my speech therapists. As she took the call on the phone at the bar, to all of our surprise, she yelled out, "A hundred dollars, I'll be right over." It seemed her husband had just won a raffle at church and wanted to notify her of his good fortune. Regrettably, she did not share the reason for her outburst with the men at the bar who still today suffer from the misconception that my income is derived from less than honorable means. It's tough to shake a bad image in a small town like that.

As the process of closing down large state institutions for the mentally retarded made progress, the concept of small community residences became exceedingly more popular. Due to the high level of services in our region combined with very affordable housing options, the state began looking at opening a number of group homes in our area. During this time, I served as the chairperson of the county committee charged with planning for such services, both programmatic and residential.

As potential home sites were selected for consideration as group homes, neighborhood residents came forward at public hearings to voice their opinions as to the feasibility of moving children with mental retardation into each particular location. In some cases their opinion caused us to reconsider, but for the most part we were able to gain acceptance for our plan. Community awareness of the nature and needs of the mentally retarded had improved considerably over time, but even I was surprised that the State had just put in a purchase offer on a small former motel two doors down from my house in Skaneateles. Anxious about how my neighbors would react to having six to eight adults with mental retardation living in our midst, I was pleased that after a public hearing our village board became the first one in Central New York to unanimously welcome such a residence into their community. With the home just seventy five feet from my front door, I felt more confident about reassuring residents of other communities about the impact such a group home would have on their neighborhood.

In the spring of 1984, just before I left the area, I received one of the most amusing phone calls of my professional career. On the other end of the line was an elderly lady who explained to me that she lived at a nursing home located about a mile north of my office.

"Say, do you offer sign language lessons for senior citizens?" she inquired of me.

Unable to answer affirmatively, I was nonetheless inquisitive about the motive behind her unique question.

"What reason do you have for asking?" I probed.

"Well, there are a lot of old women living down here and most of them are going deaf on me. I've still got a whole lot of things to say, and I thought if someone could teach us all sign language I could just keep rolling along."

"I must admit you have a great idea there, and I'll see if I can uncover some other agency which might be able to provide that service for you," I replied.

After searching a few days, I finally came up empty.

I found her creativity and spunk so very typical of the hardworking rural and blue collar natives of that area. I'm willing to bet she still has the ear of someone who is equally as intrigued by her determination as I was.

The most obvious downside of earning a living as a school administrator is the necessity to uproot one's family continually in order to proceed up the ladder of success. Thus, one is constantly haunted by the potential of sacrificing the well-being of one's children in the service of the children of others. The vagabond existence that many young principals and central office administrators have had to endure has greatly lessened the interest in such a career path toward the "higher level positions."

It was with that in mind that I remained for such a lengthy period of time in a village that offered so much to its children. Blessed with scenic beauty, excellent recreation, and outstanding schools, Skaneateles was the ideal venue in which to raise a family. Fortunately, I can only look back with pride to the type of environment I was able to provide for my three children to grow up in.

From 1973 to 1984, I was lucky enough to recruit some of the best trained and enthusiastic young special educators in the nation. While we were unable to remunerate them at a level that resulted in them becoming long term employees of the BOCES, their contributions to the educational life of our community were significant. As a result, the children with disabilities served by the Cayuga-Onondaga BOCES were most fortunate.

Living and working in the Finger Lakes Region, I had learned a lot about the meaning of such terms as "cost-effective" and "work ethic." These hardworking citizens expected a lot for their money, and they got it. They were excellent in demonstrating to their children the value of hard work and determination. If you shared their values and helped their children attain a better life, you felt their deep appreciation. More importantly, you had friends for life.

The Art and Beauty of Teaching

*T*he Boston Celtics of the 1960s and 1970s running the fast break, Harry Belafonte under the stars at Forest Hills beguiling an SRO audience, and the Bolshoi Ballet performing Swan Lake with flawless perfection stand out in my memory as human events that have resulted in awesome admiration by those fortunate enough to experience them live. As rare as such opportunities are for the average American of my generation and financial means, I was, however, blessed with the professional privilege of observing on a regular basis human activities that many times were equally as exciting and inspirational.

The determination and creativity of a teacher of young children with emotional disturbance, the patience and love expressed by the teacher of a self-abusive child with severe retardation, or the encouragement and emotional support displayed by the coach of a Special Olympian racing toward the finish line have been focal points of my professional life for many years. Charged with observing and recording the value of such interactions between special educators and their students has provided me with a deep appreciation of the art form known as special education. Unfortunately, the vast majority of this art and beauty takes place far from the view of our society at large. The burden falls upon the privileged few of us who have the unique opportunity to bear witness to these teaching adventures to articulate their meaning and to share this drama with the rest of humanity. By reflecting upon the skills I've observed demonstrated by my colleagues over the past three decades, we might all grow in our appreciation of each other's contributions to the exciting field of special education.

As we enter the 1990s, the human diversity that exists within special education continues to expand. Infants of drug addicted parents, children with profound retardation and multiple additional disabilities, academically gifted students with complex learning disabilities, and angry adolescents with behavioral disorders consistently challenge the repertoire of teaching skills and behaviors of special educators in rural, urban, and suburban settings. Responding with commitment and energy in order to meet these needs are a myriad of unique individuals whose desire to improve upon the quality of life of exceptional children manifests itself in a variety of human characteristics and teaching behaviors. The combination of these characteristics and behaviors results in the development of the skills necessary to become a successful special educator.

Having interviewed more than 2,500 individuals for positions working with exceptional children and employing nearly one thousand, I am frequently asked about the qualities I search for when seeking people who can have a positive impact on the lives of children with disabilities. After careful reflection upon this question and in consideration of the many highly skilled individuals I have observed in their classrooms over the past twenty years, a number of attributes spring to mind.

The four primary qualities I look for in a special educator are **kindness**, **intuition**, **determination**, and **sincerity**. While **kindness** is not a word we hear utilized often, my firm belief has always been that we can separate the "givers" from the "takers" in our society. In so doing we identify those whose level of human kindness would reflect itself in the quality of interaction with children with disabilities. The manifestation of this trait is crucial in building the kinds of relationships with children, their parents, and co-workers that are critical to success as a special educator.

The gift of **intuition** has been a dramatic asset to those teachers who are fortunate enough to possess such skill. With so many exceptional children, the ability to anticipate their needs or behavior in advance is crucial to the creation of a learning environment consisting of order and respect for all involved in the process. The truly intuitive teacher at work with energetic learners is highly exciting to observe, and is an exquisite form of the art of special education.

Part of the essence of being a skillful special educator is the ability to manifest **determination** in a supportive manner with children who love to challenge their teachers. Frequently, we are confronted with "reluctant learners" who have successfully defied the efforts of numerous adults to coerce or co-opt them into a positive teacher/student relationship. The skillful special educator communicates his or her determination to take whatever means are necessary to facilitate productive learning within the classroom. Witnessing the wilting impact of such perseverance upon aggressive and stubborn youngsters is most enjoyable.

Coating one's teaching style with a strong dose of **sincerity** can insure that children feel a high level of security within the special education classroom. Many of our children have been victimized by broken adult promises and, as a result, have a unique skill in detecting insincerity. The creation of trust is the backbone of the relationship between students and staff in the world of special education. Periodically, the children will administer their own sincerity test to insure that the teacher is still in their corner, and the successful special educator will always pass with flying colors.

Kindness, intuition, determination, and **sincerity** have always been my top four characteristics. Once again, my selection of these traits was dictated by what my students communicated to me were important factors to them. Ironically, when you take the initial letter of each of these attributes it spells **kids.** After all, what better way is there to describe what it is that the true special educator is all about?

Success as a teacher within the special education classroom is predicated upon many other interpersonal variables. While a number of these characteristics are individual in nature and may relate directly to the age and disability of the students, there is one combination of teacher traits that is important in most every special education setting.

The blend of **structure** and **spontaneity** within the personal makeup of the teacher of exceptional children is a high predictor of success. So many of our children come from environments devoid of consistency that they respond favorably to adults who can determine with a high degree of certainty what their school day will be like. Therefore, a teacher who has a high awareness of where the students are, where he or she needs to take them, and the proper rate of learning will provide a level of structure conducive to instructional success. Resulting from this favorable routine will be a strong sense of security which, in turn, creates a learning environment with the potential to promote trust and improve self concept.

However, as well structured and consistent as one may be, children with disabilities don't always respond in a highly predictable fashion. As a result, the special educator also needs to posses a level of spontaneity equal to the challenges his or her students may present. Calm under fire, he or she responds to the unanticipated in a manner that convinces the students the he or she is a paragon of flexibility and that our beloved structure will return to the classroom momentarily. The combination of these two characteristics form the pedagogical foundation for the development of a career as a successful special educator.

My role as interviewer in the process of hiring a candidate for a special education teaching position holds within it a certain set of responsibilities of which I am acutely aware. Having many years ago made the conscious decision that I could better impact the system from a leadership position, my influence on the children may entirely depend upon the quality of people I employ. Their daily contact with students must somehow exemplify the value system that was so meaningful to me during those years I spent as a classroom teacher. Currently I have two layers of professionals (principals and teachers) between me and the children, so that this challenge is even more complex.

With this in mind, the time I spend in interpersonal contact with potential employees holds added meaning. During those crucial minutes, I probe for an additional critical characteristic that is indicative of success in our field.

Strength of character is a concept that in all reality is difficult to define. Searching for it in the interview requires developing a dialogue and relationship where the value clarification process can take place in a meaningful manner. When taken cumulatively, the primary four characteristics described earlier result in a formula for determining strength of character. Can this individual serve as an attitudinal change agent relative to people's value of how our society deals with individual difference? Is he or she someone who can motivate others to take risks with exceptional children? Does the candidate project the ability to instill in children with disabilities confidence that he or she can assist them in hurdling the barriers to success and happiness?

To admit that the answers to these questions are derived from anything other than instinct would be less than truthful. However, gut instinct as it relates to determining strength of character may well be the most critical variable in selecting vigorous and effective professionals for the field of special education.

As anyone entering the education profession must invariably do, the new special educator must reflect upon those personality characteristics that seem to be effective with the type of children being served. In so doing, it is important to remember that the safety and security needs of the students may well be a critical dynamic in how they perceive their teachers. Due to the wide variety of less than nurturing experiences some students may have had during their early childhood, they look to their teacher to provide a safe and consistently caring environment in which they can learn, grow, and sometimes take risks.

In my first few weeks working with the children at the House of Providence, I became acutely aware of what they wanted from me. Very simply, they needed to know that if another child in the group lost control of himself, I was capable of protecting them from him. The flip side of the equation also needed to be apparent. Should they lose control of themselves, would I be capable of cooling them down without inflicting pain or embarrassment? I quickly learned how important it was to insure that a child, no matter how outrageous or inappropriate his behavior, be given the opportunity to save face. A teacher, cognizant of these safety and security needs, will create a strong basic foundation for building a dynamic and effective instructional program.

Having earlier mentioned the value of structure for a special educator, I would like to raise a point of caution in this implementation. There are those teachers whose level of regimentation and lack of personal warmth cause the observer to question for whose benefit is the structure being provided? Students sit quietly at their desks, performing one academic task after another. Their level of productivity and growth in basic skills is impressive. The lack of affect by both the students and the teacher during the teaching/learning process is rather dramatic. Usually, the teacher will rationalize that "this is obviously the way this type of student best learns."

Over time, the students being served by this style of teacher become dependent on the structure for their learning success while failing to develop the interpersonal controls and social skills necessary to function in other learning environments. Therefore, as every successful teacher knows, it is important to regularly assess the degree of structure being provided for the students and adjust relative to the changing needs of the children being served. Only then can we all feel secure that the structure within the classroom is one hundred percent for the benefit of the children.

"Tell me about the quality of your *listening skills* in the classroom." The reaction I get to this question in an interview leads me to believe that this important area of teaching may well be under emphasized in our schools today. Most of us enter the special education classroom eager to help and impart knowledge to our young charges. Sometimes, however, we forget that the children come to school each day with things important to them that they wish to communicate to their teacher.

Many of our students experience neurological and/or speech difficulties that tax our patience in the listening process. If we listen carefully, there are occasions when verbal feedback from our children can cause us to reflect upon the need to alter our own teaching style. Children who are aware that their teacher is an eager and willing listener come to school happier and more secure. As a result, the learning environment becomes considerably more conducive to meeting both the educational and emotional needs of the children.

Having worked with children in one form or another for over thirty years, my strongest personal belief is children either live up or down to your expectations. **Expectation theory**, if you will, is the most crucial element in the success or failure of our educational programs at all levels. Numerous books and articles have been written about how our once high educational standards have deteriorated through the process of negotiation for lesser expectations on students at all levels. While not wishing to jump onto that bandwagon, I do wish to stress that even exceptional children who manifest a variety of disabilities are capable of coercing their teachers into lowering their expectations for performance.

Realistic and flexible expectations for student output and growth reflect themselves in instructional programs that appropriately challenge exceptional children to reach the level of success they are capable of. The skillful teachers will constantly review the levels of demands they place on their students to insure that the productivity of the teacher and children is optimal.

In looking at why teachers within the regular education system fail with many students who ultimately find success in special education programs, I have come to an interesting conclusion. The skillful and well trained special educator frequently possesses the ability to nurture the students through the expectations he or she places upon them. The ability to communicate caring, while simultaneously lifting the jump bar, contrasts dramatically with the sense of failure and frustration that was so ever-present within the regular education system. Careful planning combined with relationship building with the students brings this talent to the forefront of the skillful special educator's repertoire of teaching characteristics.

Frequently, children with disabilities go through a developmental stage in their lives when they find themselves attempting to lower the expectations of adults by taking advantage of the human tendency to feel sorry for them. The successful special education teacher avoids falling into this trap which only reinforces the behavior and greatly limits the child's potential for educational and emotional growth. Creating within the classroom an environment devoid of psychological acceptance of disabling conditions results in a relationship between the teacher and his or her students built upon children's abilities and strengths. This emphasis on the positive factors they each bring into the learning process results in a joyful classroom where nurturing, growth and success abound.

As one of the most famous teachers in the history of Broadway, Anna, in **The King and I,** sings about the necessity of "Getting to Know You." Nowhere is this more applicable than for the special education teacher whose class is made up of children displaying a wide array of human diversity. Their struggle with childhood, compounded by large doses of failure, frequently result in learning and survival strategies of significant complexity. Getting to know each student and appreciating his or her uniqueness require ongoing effort and careful observation. The teacher who can predict the outcomes and consequences of his or her teaching behaviors stands a far greater chance of achieving goals in the special education classroom. Truly knowing the children dramatically reduces unanticipated consequences that teachers and children deal with daily.

In Rochester, there is a very successful magnet school whose name well reflects the nature of special education. It is called "The World of Inquiry" which aptly describes the environment special educators regularly find themselves in. Talented teachers of exceptional children frequently find themselves challenged by the uniqueness of their students' learning styles. Ever the detective, they strive to discover new techniques or materials that will open doors previously shut and bolted by reluctant or disabled learners. Constantly discussing the individual needs of each of their students with whoever is willing to listen, they seek out fresh ideas whose merit might provide them with the ultimate success - improved student learning or behavior. These inquisitive practitioners thrive on the multiplicity of unique challenges offered by special education and in return form the backbone of our profession.

The characteristics of successful teachers can only result in the art and beauty of teaching if they are appropriately reflected in the quality of the learning environment. The development of this supportive ambiance results in an educational milieu that finds even the most suspicious learner eagerly entering the classroom each morning. Far too few educators appreciate the classroom as an extension of their teaching personality. By structuring and designing this space to appropriately draw upon positive teaching characteristics, the special educator projects warmth, support, and the availability of success experiences to the children he or she works with. In so doing, many of the unique needs the children bring with them to school each day are appropriately addressed.

Once the instructional environment has been adequately created, the special educator next must address how he or she can interrelate with the students in such a manner as to make them feel good about themselves. So many of the children we find ourselves working with carry a long history of failure experiences with them as they enter our educational programs. The skillful special education teacher constantly looks for ways to point out to a child his or her self worth. By demonstrating a sincere respect for each child in a consistent manner, long standing attitudes of worthlessness slowly diminish and small amounts of self-confidence begin to evolve. Nourishing this seed with realistic and deserved positive feedback, the special educator slowly turns the corner of creating positive self-images for the students. Exciting to watch, it is even more beautiful to participate in, and is a critical factor in why people turn to special education as a career choice.

Earlier in this chapter, I mentioned the value of determination as a successful characteristic for teachers of exceptional children. With many of our children this trait may more effectively be translated into something more common to their knowledge base - stubbornness. Skillful themselves, at displaying obstinacy toward learning tasks or adults in general, many students will relate well to their teacher's stubborn persistence that they complete their work in an acceptable manner. This display of tenacity communicates a level of caring that children can identify with, given the simplicity of its manifestation. As psychologically draining as such activity can be, it is a crucial trait closely related to effectiveness in the special education classroom.

Openness to and comfort in dealing with the entire spectrum of emotions manifested by exceptional children is certainly one of the primary characteristics required for those entering the field of special education. The willingness to risk exposing one's own feelings and emotions in front of others, while at the same time being comfortable responding to the emotional needs of behaviorally-complex children, is a tall order. Those proficient in this regard quickly earn the personal and professional respect they deserve.

Special educators, such as these, are careful to display their emotions as a teaching device pro-actively in a manner consistent with appropriate adult behavior. For many of our students it is rare that they have such an opportunity at home or in the community.

On the other hand, the ability of the teacher of children with behavioral disorders to respond in a reactive mode to spontaneous outbursts while keeping a calm and comforting level of emotionality is equally challenging. A critical success factor in such instances is the teacher's ability to insure a safe and face-saving solution to resolving the incident. When such students feel comfortable that the adult responsible for providing them with external control over their emotions is caring, consistent, insightful, and effective, the disruptive impact of such occurrences is significantly diminished.

During the course of every school day there are a variety of other adults who play a critical role in the effectiveness of the special education teacher with their students. Parents, the bus driver, the principal, special subject area teachers, the lady in the lunch room, and the assistant principal for student discipline are just a few of those whose appearance on the educational stage can impact on quality performance. The artful special educator is skilled in manipulating the behavior of all such actors in a manner that supports the goals with the children he or she serves. Getting each of them on board and knowledgeable about the needs of the children, he or she surrounds the students with a school community that clearly embraces their right to pursue success in the least restrictive environment.

As positive as all these teaching characteristics are, I feel obligated to caution that there are some personal and psychological factors that special education teachers need to avoid. First is the tendency to accept the image of "miracle worker" relative to teaching difficult children.

Regular education personnel have a need to rationalize their inability to teach, or disinterest in serving, exceptional children by projecting upon special educators certain traits that no one should expect them to possess. While this may at first appear to be flattering, it can be counter productive for both the special education teacher and the students he or she serves.

As a result of this imagery, the special education teacher can find himself or herself being called upon to deal with students and issues that may not be legitimately within their purview. Unrealistic expectations by the regular education system can quickly diminish the joy and satisfaction inherent in working with exceptional children. At the same time, this type of role misinterpretation allows regular education staff to distance themselves from the "atypical learners" taught by the special education teacher. This serves as a restraining force in facilitating meaningful mainstreaming of children who are able to benefit from such interaction with their non-disabled peers. While the special educator should always be proud of what can be accomplished with their students, they must always dispel the myth of possessing a unique bag of magic tricks.

Secondly, stress and burnout are two terms that became part of our educational lexicon during the past decade. Nowhere are they more relevant than in the field of special education, particularly with those personnel who work regularly with the severely retarded or the emotionally disturbed.

I think the impact of this phenomena was best pointed out to me by a young teacher of elementary school children with emotional disturbances who, after three years in the classroom, explained to me that "her well was dry." The students kept taking and she kept giving until the point arrived at which she felt the need to request a transfer to replenish her supply of love and caring before returning to work with this type of child.

It is important that special education teachers and

their administrators recognize this need when it arises and have available to them recourse to healthy alternatives. Much has been done recently in the area of stress reduction. Our special education system needs to utilize these resources to insure that our teachers are entering their classrooms at full capacity.

The special education teachers I have known over the years have been effective with exceptional children by drawing upon relatively high amounts of **energy, enthusiasm**, and **hope**. Active within the classroom, they move about with a demeanor communicating their readiness to deal with the everyday challenges inherent with their position. Their enthusiasm for taking part in the learning process is contagious and their students sense that success experiences are close at hand. Optimistic by nature, they convey to both their students and other adults a message through their behavior, of hope for a better future for those children for whom failure has been all too prevalent.

The final two characteristics that I feel compelled to cite when reflecting upon my years of classroom observation are really the frosting on the cake. This tandem of traits, when possessed by a skilled special education teacher, magnifies the impact of his or her other qualities in such a manner as to insure beautiful learning experiences for children. **Resourcefulness** and **creativity**, in combination, result in exciting lessons perceptively designed to draw out from students maximum learning productivity. Bearing witness to such educational activities provides a feeling of exhilaration that cannot be replicated anywhere in the field of education. Matching the highest quality teachers with the students most in need of their professional attributes is what special education is all about.

Fairness would dictate that one could certainly not expect every candidate for a special education teaching position to possess the personal characteristics I just detailed. Fortunately, many of the young people entering our field do reflect many of these attributes in varying degrees. But more importantly they have been trained to utilize these traits in concert with teaching behaviors that have proven successful with exceptional children. These behaviors or strategies, easily observable, form the foundation for a well run special education classroom. By reflecting upon these pedagogical approaches to the art of teaching exceptional children we can greater appreciate the beauty of this experience.

Creating a high level of **teacher presence** within the special education classroom is the singular most effective strategy for those embarking upon our profession. The students must feel that sense of proximate support for both their academic and emotional needs. Teachers who convey this sense effectively, spend very little time dealing with off task behavior by students. Even when the teacher may have to leave the classroom for a short period of time, the aura of his or her values still pervades the learning environment and the children respond appropriately. The development of an educational milieu built around this factor is highly contributory to the ultimate success of both the teacher and his or her students.

Directly related to the creation of a high level of teacher presence is the designation of the various learning stations within the classroom. Of paramount importance is the location of these centers in such a manner as to facilitate for the teacher the opportunity to maintain both **visual** and **verbal control** over the classroom as a whole. When working with small reading groups in the rear of the classroom, the teacher should be able to observe all other students and verbally respond to their activity if necessary. Frequently, beginning teachers will sit with their back to the rest of the class and wonder why the noise level and off task behavior increases. By simply changing their position at the reading table, they immediately gain a far superior level of presence throughout the entire classroom.

From the first day you enter the special education classroom, you become vulnerable to an occupational hazard that is rarely diagnosed properly. **Negotiating with kids** can become as prevalent or as limited as your skills and value system wish it to be. Skilled beyond their years at manipulating the behavior of adults, many of our students thrive on their ability to limit the expectations placed upon them. Fairness and consistency should be the driving forces in determining a strategy whose result should be the teacher's satisfaction that all the students are working up to their potential.

The special education classroom needs to be intriguing and somewhat seductive in order to fascinate the most reluctant of learners. "Exploration allowed" should be a philosophical tenet that the teacher's behavior reflects. Learning can and should be fun, and the discovery method is, of its very nature, most efficacious with children who have experienced consistent failure. Learning by doing introduces to children a concrete learning style they can build upon throughout their lifetime.

In many special education classrooms across the country, the special education classroom teacher has the availability of paraprofessional support. The concept of teacher aides as a valuable resource to both the teacher and the students is widely accepted. It then becomes incumbent upon the teacher to insure that the **utilization of the tag team partner** reflects itself in increased opportunities for student academic and social growth. Having observed hundreds of paraprofessionals at work, I am sensitive to the need for creativity and communication in their appropriate deployment. When teacher and aide are suitably in sync and complement each other, the rate of learning within the program expands significantly.

In its most simplistic form, success in the special education classroom is derived by combining behavior management skills with sound and creative instructional strategies. Before the academic tasks can be addressed, the teacher must have created an instructional environment where respect for learning and for the rights of each other is obvious. The question the trained observer must ask in the special education classroom is, "Do the students appear to understand what is expected of them and what the consequences of their behavior will be?"

Designing the classroom behavior rules to best fit the needs and functional level of the students is critical to the success potential of both teacher and students. Each student must take ownership in the development of these standards, so that when they become practice there will be a minimum of quibbling over interpretation. The teacher, therefore, needs to actively involve the students in deciding upon the behavioral norms that will be enforced within the classroom.

Once the rules have been accepted, it becomes the teacher's responsibility to enforce these regulations consistently so as to reinforce their importance in the regular operation of the classroom. Gradually these norms become inculcated into the value system of the students and many of the children begin self-policing their own behavior. When this process occurs, the teacher's potential to increase academic time on task multiplies significantly.

There are a wide variety of behavior management systems that have been proven effective within special education. Selecting which of these techniques to utilize should always depend on the combination of the teacher's style and the students needs. Frequently, philosophical issues come into play, as well as the degree of parent and principal support available within the process. While consistency in implementation is paramount, it is also important to recognize that instances may arise where individual needs may dictate exceptions to the rule. Therefore, flexibility should be a consideration when selecting or developing a behavior management system for utilization within the special education setting.

The most successful special educators are those who have at their immediate disposal a wide array of behavior management skills to draw upon, either pro-actively or reactively, with children who manifest behavioral disorders. Many years ago, our late colleague, Fritz Redl, categorized these strategies and described them in such a manner that they have become for many the foundation of sound behavior management within our field. Such terms as **planned ignoring**, **signal interference**, **proximity** and **touch control**, and **antiseptic bouncing** have become skills special educators attempt to master. His contributions to the literature in the field of emotional disturbance are among the most significant of the past half century. Reading about his experiences with children with severe behavioral disorders is entertaining, thought provoking, and inspirational.

With the class rules and the carefully selected behavior management system in place, the skilled special education teacher has now created an environment where instructional issues may be thoroughly addressed. Successfully modifying the surface behavior of the students, the teacher must now avoid the tendency to ignore the fact that the students might wish to change the teacher's behavior. Drawing upon finely tuned listening skills, the teacher must encourage a realistic amount of student feedback about the efficacy of the system. Much of this feedback may be nonverbal in nature and will require careful data collection and analysis.

After processing this feedback, the talented teacher must wrestle with a difficult question. How should I change my teaching style to accommodate the needs of my students, and is such a change in all of our best interests? It is rare that the regular education teacher is called upon to contemplate such an issue, but special educators deal with this conundrum frequently. It takes a true professional to deal with this issue, but like so much in our business, it comes with the territory.

Earlier I discussed some of the potential problems involved with over-negotiating with students, but there is an alternative technique proven useful in some special education programs. **Student contracting** allows the teacher and each student to jointly determine the quantity and quality of learning productivity that should result over an agreed upon period of time. Tied into the contract are usually rewards or penalties that will result from the completion or breaking of that agreement. Most often this technique is utilized with secondary level students who need a concrete and continuous reward system in order to motivate them to extend their academic efforts. The teacher needs to feel in control of this process, and should regularly attempt to increase expectations and lower the rewards as students discover some form of intrinsic reward in their academic successes.

As with all behavior management techniques, it is imperative that the reward system selected by the teacher be one that is consistent with the value system and developmental level of the students. It is not uncommon to see rewards for student behavior that vary from breakfast cereal to cigarettes or money. Given the expanding diversity of children that we serve, designing creative and effective rewards can be most challenging. Careful consultation with parents and the school clinician should take place prior to the development of any reward system.

It should always be remembered, however, that while food, field trips, and toys can be effective in obtaining instructional and behavioral objectives, we must always strive to make the sense of accomplishment the ultimate motivator for our children's participation in the learning process. Setting up unrealistic or artificial rewards that have no basis in regular education or the real world only compounds the potential impact of our children's disabilities.

Teachers, whose behavior management systems are most instructionally effective, are those who have best been able to clearly communicate to their students the consequences of their behavior. Much of this communication can be non-directive or even non-verbal. A comment such as, "I like the way Billy is sitting so quietly and doing his seat work" tells those who are getting restless in the class more than it does Billy. A raised eyebrow or a pointed finger may be all it takes to return some children to task.

Classrooms where children are adequately aware of

how their or their fellow student's behavior will be dealt with are classrooms where the potential for academic growth is the highest. Observing teachers skillfully controlling the quality of human interactions in these educational environments is a prime example of both the art and beauty of special education teaching.

The next step on the road to success as a special educator is then to take advantage of the educational milieu that has been developed and create opportunities for students to work together productively toward common goals. These goals may be either academic or social in nature, or both. Learning to work together with others in a mutually productive manner is a lifetime skill that too often we overlook.

The skillful special educator is aware of which of the students can be matched in order to maximize the benefits of **pupil teaming**. Creatively designed activities in the classroom or in the community lend themselves to social skill development. Too often, we address the issue of correcting or eliminating inappropriate behavior without taking the time to teach appropriate social skills. To the degree that the teacher wishes to make it such, the classroom becomes a laboratory for children to test out their newly discovered social skills with their peers. Eventually this process leads to creating similar social interactions with non-disabled children in regular education classes. We must avoid the natural tendency to overemphasize the need for academic remediation in special education and balance our program with a variety of meaningful social learning activities.

A key skill for special education teachers to master is that of effectively **serving as an advocate** for their students. Throughout their school lives these children have been looked at negatively by the adults working within the system. Children who differ, pose a threat to those who desire to rid their professional lives of unnecessary complexity. It therefore becomes incumbent upon the special education teacher to facilitate attitudinal change with staff throughout the school.

By carefully designing social activities or team-teaching, the special class teacher can demonstrate the abilities that the students possess rather than their disabilities. By giving other adults in the school the opportunity to experience success with children with disabilities, you soon discover that they become less reluctant to work with them. At the same time the students are learning how to sell themselves as capable learners who deserve to be valued in the school setting. When regular education staff internalize the fact that their students accept children with disabilities, they begin to realize that human potential can be measured in a variety of ways. This advocacy role for the special educator is critical in broadening the school-wide support base for the children they serve.

Due to the nature of the challenges implicit in teaching exceptional children, when the teacher has developed a successful teaching style he or she has a tendency to stick with it. A pattern emerges of consistent learning activities to which the students regularly respond in a positive mode. The teacher, the students and their parents all appreciate the steady growth that is taking place.

Let us just imagine that at a two day professional conference he or she just attended, our special education teacher found himself or herself excited about a number of new instructional approaches which would require him or her to make some rather significant changes in his or her teaching style. Suddenly, the issue of risk taking causes a process of professional soul-searching to take place.

Why change if things are going so well? Can the children deal with the changes that I want to have take place? What if I fail and then have trouble returning to my old proven methodology?

Such **risk taking** usually results in professional and student growth if done gradually. Careful assessment of the ongoing impact of the changes will guide the teacher throughout the process. The more varied the methodology of the special education teacher, the more capable the students become in adapting their learning styles to teachers they will relate to in the future. If the decision has to be made to return to the old tried and true teaching style, no one will welcome it more than the children who have flourished under it. Risk taking does require courage and insight, but its long range impact on both the teacher and the students is well worth it.

If, in fact, *variety* is the spice of life, the skilled special educator knows how to best season the classroom. It is imperative that each day children take part in a variety of learning activities. Individual, small group, and full class instructional experiences should be available on a regular basis. Seat work assignments should be provided that result in a variety of tasks with differing challenges. We must never underestimate our student's potential for boredom, because, in concert with their other learning problems, it can be devastating.

With the technology and media available to classroom teachers today, there are virtually no limits to creating instructional diversity. Knowing this, the skillful special educator prepares learning experiences which excite children with the joy of learning. Teaching our students to utilize the learning tools they have available to them is the best method we have of preparing them for the challenges of the next century.

Many of the professional positions within the field of special education require the ability to work effectively with other adults. Teachers of the severely disabled must direct the work activities of a number of paraprofessionals while at the same time working closely with a variety of therapists who work with their students. A teacher of children with emotional disturbances works side by side with a counselor and a crisis intervention teacher. Their ability to communicate is critical to the effectiveness of the program. Multi-disciplinary and trans-disciplinary staff configurations are common program designs which place strong emphasis on professionals to effectively interact.

The day of the special education teacher alone in the classroom, working far from the view of others, is long gone. The skilled special educator welcomes the support for himself or herself and his or her students, and utilizes the unique skills that each discipline brings to bear. Team meetings offer the opportunity to share information, brainstorm strategies, and evaluate student progress. Differences of opinion must be resolved to the satisfaction of the entire team and the special education teacher as the captain must insure that the entire process is one that maximizes the potential for student and staff success. While these skills have never been the focus of special education teacher training programs, their mastery is critical to the success of many special educators.

Having observed the amount of professional growth demonstrated by special education teachers during the first five years of their teaching careers, I am considerably impressed by the importance of this stage of their career. In order to maximize their potential for success in this challenging profession, adequacy of, and openness to, supervision and constructive feedback is critical. Professional circles and peer observation provide methods for beginning teachers to discuss the numerous issues they face during the formative stage of their professional development. Supervisory practices that reward openness and inquiry result in the evolution of teaching styles and behaviors that result in successful classroom practices.

Mentor teachers and buddies for newcomers to the field can provide reassurance for eager young teachers whose commitment to success may cause them to be overly self-critical. Video and/or audio taping of carefully selected lessons frequently offer peers the opportunity to learn from each other. In concert with supervision from appropriately trained special education administrators, these techniques can provide the support necessary during the most dynamic and influential period of a teacher's career.

A concept that is often lost in our need to attend to so

many other factors within the classroom is the importance of **modeling as a teaching behavior**. Many special educators lose sight of how important they are in the eyes of their students. For many of the children, the teacher is the most significant adult in their young lives. As a result, these students hold high expectations for their teachers and eagerly model behavior that is consistent with these expectations.

Few special educators are totally comfortable dealing with this concept because it adds an even higher level of responsibility to an already difficult job. Observing how frequently children respond to the positive human qualities manifested by their teachers, I feel strongly that the potential for utilizing this power for the positive benefit of children should never be underestimated.

A major belief among experts in the field of education today is centered around the concept of the teacher as **decision maker**. Major efforts in professional staff development have focused on the ability of classroom practitioners to constantly make decisions which result in teaching behaviors that will positively impact upon the learning process. The validity of this concept multiplies dramatically when applied to the special educator.

Given the amount of academic and behavioral diversity contained within the special education classroom, the ability of the teacher to collect data, analyze it, and make spontaneous decisions is severely tested in an ongoing manner. Billy is experiencing difficulty with his math problems; Sam is starting to act up in the back of the room; and Mary just informed you that she forgot to take her epilepsy medication this morning. Average day at the office, but in reality only one minute of a six hour school day.

The skilled special education teacher is called upon to make significantly more and more complex decisions than any of their regular education counterparts. The knowledge and understanding of students, combined with mastery of the teaching techniques we've been discussing, allow teachers to make decisions resulting in responses that insure successful student experiences.

Among the more successful special educators are those who utilize multi-sensory instructional techniques throughout the school day. Long after completing my formal education, I became aware that I had much better auditory memory than visual memory. If my teachers had known that, I'm sure it wouldn't have changed their teaching style one iota. The skilled teacher of exceptional children however, armed with this information, offers the students a variety of learning modalities in order to take advantage of the strengths they possess.

With students manifesting severe mental retardation or multiple handicaps, sensory stimulation and data collection is a vital component of their educational program. Breakthroughs in technology have given special educators and related therapists new strategies to draw upon with these children. The ability of the teacher to design the program around factors reflective of multi-sensory awareness is a fundamental skill.

Carrying this concept one step further, there has been considerable research resulting in more effective methods of diagnosing the learning styles of various students. Equipped with this ability, the teacher of exceptional children can design teaching strategies that allow for the uniqueness in learning styles within the classroom. Matching the teaching style with the student's learning style creates instructional opportunities rarely considered within the regular education system.

Such efforts require careful planning, the availability of a variety of instructional materials, the assistance of a paraprofessional, and feedback from a school psychologist. The value of such an instructional program is in its flexibility, degree of individualization, and the potential for successful learning experiences it provides for the students.

Another teaching behavior manifested by talented educators of exceptional children is the **ability to ask questions** of students in such a manner as to minimize their sense of risk taking. Learners who have experienced failure in traditional instructional settings are understandably reluctant to respond to questioning techniques which are not carefully thought out. Therefore, the special education teacher who truly knows the students will be aware with a high degree of certainly which students will be able to respond appropriately to which questions the teacher may be planning to ask during a particular lesson.

This concept reminds me of another of Fritz Redl's contributions to the lexicon of special education - that of **hurdle help**. The skillful teacher's ability to predict which questions or problems individual students may need help with allows for the teacher to be available to provide that assistance when it is needed. While never proclaiming to be an outstanding special education teacher, I am proud of the fact that I rarely asked one of my children a question in class without knowing whether or not he or she was capable of providing the correct answer. Frustration and embarrassment are rarely, if ever, effective methods of providing meaningful learning.

The final behavior exhibited by talented special educators is really in the form of a caution. All of education is sometimes prone to falling for fads or easy solutions for complex problems. Avoiding those who sell such quick fixes when working with children with learning and behavioral problems is a challenge. In the past twenty-five years, I've heard proposed and seen implemented instructional approaches, many of which defied reason, and some of which defied gravity. Teaching children with dyslexia to read by utilizing a trampoline, cutting down distractions for the learning disabled by placing each student in a stall, and the use of aversive training techniques for the behavioral disordered have caused all of us to step back and scratch our heads.

Our need to continually search for solutions must be tempered with logic and common sense. The elimination of de-humanizing methodology and the increased research on the value of new instructional technology offer today's special educators opportunities and tools that were only dreamed of years ago. When planning your instructional strategies, it always pays to ask yourself, "How would I feel if I were being asked to do this by my teacher?"

All special education teachers manifest some combination of the human characteristics and teaching skills that have been covered throughout this chapter. The impact that they have each day on the children they serve is directly related to the number of each and the degree to which they possess them. From this complicated formula comes the richness that results in the art and beauty of teaching in the special education classroom.

From my vast memory bank of instructional observation, allow me to withdraw some examples of skilled or not so skilled teachers whose work with children points out both the high points and areas in need of improvement in our profession. Each of the teaching styles reflected here is a composite but in some cases the description bears a strong resemblance to some of the outstanding practitioners I've had the honor and privilege to supervise. On the other extreme, I believe that there is something to be learned from a bad example so I will provide you with illustrations of two such well meaning, but less effective classroom models.

The Actress

Smiling and bubbly she moves around the classroom with the grace of a professional dancer. Possessing a high level of surface energy, her enthusiasm is contagious as she interfaces with her students and other school staff. Her "let me entertain you" demeanor results in happy and productive children who attend to her every movement and manifest a high need to please their teacher in return.

Utilizing voice inflection and appropriate humor, she maintains strong verbal control over the classroom which adds to her high level of teacher presence. This provides her students with a strong sense of security and predictability of learning outcomes. She thrives on the beauty of childhood (and her role in it), and communicates her strong belief in the human potential of her students to other adults within the school. When her students are eventually mainstreamed into regular education classes they prove remarkably successful.

Her strong emotional attachment to her students is communicated through her reasonable yet high expectations for them. Driven by perfection, she wants others to share her commitment to emphasizing the students capabilities rather than their disabilities. When finally having to leave her classroom, I always wanted to let out a cheer and quickly looked to find a reason for a return visit.

The Task Master

Unsure of her ability to deal effectively with the academic and emotional needs of her students, she discovers the best way to relate to them is through the continuous work assignments she provides. Seemingly not aware that "little Danny Dole died a dastardly ditto death," she keeps the machine grinding out worksheets at a rapid pace. As her students reluctantly sit at their desks (bored and squirrelly), she moves around the classroom in such a manner as to insure the continuation of on-task behavior.

Occasional verbal threats or meaningless smiley faces insure that her children will have a pile of papers each day to promote the illusion of pupil progress. The children occasionally attempt to discover the whereabouts of a warm, caring human being behind this instructional facade. When I ask about a certain student, her response is related to his academic productively or behavioral activity.

While this style of teacher may well desire to relate differently to her students, she lacks the courage to take the risks necessary to proceed. She comes to rationalize her style as one that creates student growth whatever the potential negative side effect. Facilitating change with this type of teacher is a lengthy process but one certainly deserving of the effort.

The Learning Center's Ringmaster

Her classroom is epitomized by considerable teacher and student movement. A variety of creative and well kept instructional venues located throughout the room welcomes and entices curious learners. Knowledgeable about the latest methods and materials, she utilizes them to encourage and reward student involvement. Her learning activities are always child centered and are delivered in such a fashion so as to promote a sense of mutual respect.

Pupil teaming, in small and large group instructional options are always available, and there is an air of excitement within the classroom. Utilizing verbal support and rewards as appropriate, she directs students to areas where they stand a strong chance of meeting with success. Classroom technology gives ample evidence that it is frequently a part of the regular instructional environment.

She makes excellent use of her paraprofessional support in preparation and in providing students with feedback about their work. The children feel good about themselves as learners and are confident that they can respond effectively to a variety of instructional challenges and teaching styles.

Careful to address the affective as well as the cognitive domain, she cares deeply about the children and demonstrates it by showering them with success while constantly lifting the jump bar. Her professional and personal relationships with her colleagues are excellent and they accept her students as they do their own. This human dynamo well knows the meaning of the term "TGIF."

The Pal

His claim to fame as a special educator centers around his relationship building skills. Students appear to like him but after further examination it is discovered that they like him primarily because he has developed friendship through low expectations for student productivity. A skilled negotiator, he cuts deals with his students that allow everyone to get along just fine. Behavior problems are rare because there is little opportunity for conflict. This of course pleases the school principal who reciprocates by keeping his distance from the program.

Curriculum decisions are based upon what workbooks, newspapers, and other commercial materials might suggest that they would keep the students happy and entertained. Parents demonstrate support for his commitment based upon their child's willingness to go to school each day. In addition, they are rarely asked to help with homework or get involved beyond their level of interest. Staff within the school marvel at the great rapport he has with his students who were never considered to possess much academic potential anyway.

Gradually student boredom begins to set in and with it lower self-esteem. Possessing limited behavior management skills, the relationship with the students becomes strained. Attempting to counter this trend by increasing the work load, he meets head on with pupil resistance. With limited resources and only a one dimensional teaching style to fall back on, panic begins to set in. Now is the time to pass blame. Will it be certain students who need to be removed from the class or is the fault with the poor support provided by his supervisor and principal?

The Role Models

"Once in every life, someone comes along," - so sang Ronnie Milsap. I guess I've just been very fortunate to have selected special education for my life's work because I've had the unique opportunity to hire and supervise a number of young energetic teachers who were as close to perfection in the classroom as anyone could hope for. Insightful, caring, and with such strength of character, they would instill in their students a sense of self worth resulting in a classroom ambiance radiating with joy and success. The children hang on their teacher's every word and overflow with eagerness to attack the next learning activity.

The warmth of her smile signalled the children that there was no other place she would rather be. Communicating to them her value for them as learners, she effortlessly reinforces their appropriate behavior almost by habit. They know that she knew, and if she thought they could then they would. With a seemingly endless supply of nurturing teaching behaviors, the environment she created abounded in peacefulness and success.

An example of this type of teacher entered my office in Auburn one day just passing through town on his way to Michigan. Knowing no one in the area, he wanted the opportunity to talk that summer afternoon with someone who shared his interest in special education. Two hours later we had arranged for him to come back again to join our staff and teach one of our most difficult classes.

I was first taken by his gentle nature, but his students soon learned that his commitment to them created in him a self-expectation that fueled his drive for perfection as a special educator. Patient, highly organized, and possessing an ever increasing skill at designing fun filled learning activities, he quickly established a relationship with his students that was both unique and beautiful. Desperately in need of a healthy male role model, the boys in the class were in awe of their teacher, and when their success reflected his success a most fortuitous cycle came into being. Watching both teacher and students growing and thriving together in the learning process was one of the most joyous experiences of my professional life.

Teachers like Claire and Mike don't come along very often but when they do, you hope that the band begins playing "Send in the Clones."

It was not my intent in any way to imply that in order to be successful as a special educator one must possess all or even many of the characteristics and skills previously considered. These reflections upon traits, which were in reality possessed by hundreds of different special education teachers, were offered to help us better understand why some individuals succeed so effectively with children with whom others have failed so miserably. Having been given the opportunity to invade their professional privacy, I owe it to those wonderful examples of our profession to pass down the legacy of their cumulative skills.

Special education in it purist form is a beautiful art. All of us on this earth are hopefully involved in the pursuit of happiness. For so many of us who have the pleasure of working with exceptional children, that search has ended in the special education classroom.

Questions in Search of Answers

*D*uring the decades of the '60s, '70s, and '80s, Americans involved with the disabled struggled with a plethora of issues related to the creation of alternative service delivery systems for exceptional individuals. The search for human and fiscal resources was an ongoing challenge that took up considerable time and energy. The evolution of governance, legislation, and regulations necessitated great debates among proponents of alternate solutions to common problems.

As our awareness of the impact of various disabilities became more acute, we grappled with methods for best meeting the needs of these children. Research and practice resulted in the discovery of pedagogy that intensified the debate involving professors and practitioners relative to how children with various disabilities should be taught.

Arguments over the meaning of least restrictive environment, and whether mainstreaming was myth or magnificent, were extremely emotional and impacted on many programs. The results of these debates have had cultural implications that have been long lasting within communities throughout the nation.

The movement of those with mental retardation from decadent institutions into normal community settings stirred a cauldron of feelings that resulted in a moral soul searching for many of our citizenry. Public meetings were emotionally charged, and, in some cases, violence confronted those advocating for such change. Decades of misunderstanding were difficult to overcome when a sudden recognition of the need for a major philosophical and programmatic change of course became apparent.

The process of labeling children, racial bias in the procedure for measuring intelligence, and the concept of zero rejection were issues that excited parents, professionals, and public policy makers with equal degrees of intensity. Attempting to successfully negotiate solutions to those problems was, and will continue to be, a lengthy drawn out process with strong feelings abundantly expressed. The need to continue this dialogue however is extremely important to the sociological and educational future

168

of our nation.

While all these heated discussions were taking place in the halls of academia or in school board rooms across the country, enthusiastic and energetic special educators were quietly and with great determination, on a daily basis, attempting to improve the human condition for exceptional children. It was the efforts of these educators that the researchers were studying and that board members were taking pride in as they attempted to evolve public policy within special education.

When federal and state bureaucrats joined with professional and advocacy groups to implore legislators to change the legal foundation for special education, it was with confidence that what was happening, and could happen, within the special education classroom would be worth the additional billions of dollars they were seeking. Confirmation of this belief has certainly been forthcoming and increased expenditures have been matched by the enthusiastic support parents have demonstrated for special education programs which have successfully met the unique needs of their children.

A retrospective review of the past three decades may well lead one to mistakenly expect that the major issues within special education have been raised and dealt with by those who have been the impact players during that era. While much of this conclusion may be valid, there still remains a necessity to create closure on many of these items. More importantly, the evolution of the system of education for children with disabilities has by its very nature raised an entire new series of questions that will confront those who embrace our profession during the decade and the century just ahead.

The solution to these problems will require the involvement of many factions within our society, and they challenge special educators to instill their value system into the moral and educational fabric of our nation. The answers to these questions will need to be worked out at varied levels (federal, state, local) and a consensus will be difficult to reach. The need to solve these dilemmas is crucial to determining whether the progress of the preceding three decades will result in the reality so many have dreamed of.

Whenever I contemplate the future of special education, a number of questions concern me. It is my desire to be a part of the dialogue that must take place relative to these issues. My hope is that we will be able to entice some of this nation's finest individuals to become stakeholders in this process. Then, and only then, will our solutions eliminate the final roadblocks to the full inclusion of our disabled citizens into the mainstream of American society.

Many of these questions may, at first blush, appear to paint a rather negative picture of our current society. It is important, though, to appreciate how far we have come and to understand that many of the solutions have been consistently evolving and may be within easy reach. Traveling throughout our nation today, one is constantly bombarded by the impact that public policy has had on the disabled during the latter third of this century. Our momentum continues to grow, and I am highly optimistic that the answers to the challenges remaining are well within our grasp.

With each question that I raise, I will attempt to explain in some depth why my level of concern has been exacerbated. In addition, I will provide some suggestions as to what course of action might result in our arrival at potential solutions. Recognizing my potential for fallibility, I nonetheless plunge forward with the intent of encouraging much needed discussion on issues which are critical to the well being of exceptional children in the years ahead.

Question #1

In a global economy, will the human values inherent in special education be compromised in order to compete financially with other cultures?

Recently we have become more aware of the fact that a dramatic shift has taken place in the worldwide business arena. The economic health of our nation is being threatened by a wide variety of foreign competitors whose labor market is dramatically different than our own. Many of our own corporate giants are accessing that cheaper labor market themselves in an attempt to compete effectively in the open market.

Meanwhile, at home, advocates for workers with disabilities are frustrated by the inordinately high unemployment rate among those they serve. Pay scales for the disabled have risen very little, and now with

170

increased technology, the threat of taking these jobs onto foreign territory in order to be more cost effective looms large.

Special education and vocational training for students with disabilities is a costly enterprise. It has historically been justified because of the potential it holds for making its graduates self-sufficient. Should a dramatic shift in the availability of gainful employment take place, questions could arise about the return on society's investment in disabled individuals. An economic Cold War could panic policy makers into considering re-allocation of resources into populations whose potential for productivity could be considerably higher.

This scenario, frightening as it may seem, must be contemplated by those who desire to advocate for exceptional children in the years ahead. The value of human life and the potential of each individual to learn and grow must become more deeply inculcated into our culture. Therefore, economic considerations will not become the overriding criteria upon which future decisions of resource allocations are made. By working with the non-disabled children in our schools to promulgate the beliefs that form the foundation of special education, we will be able to develop an enlightened citizenry on issues revolving around human worth. In so doing, the thought of sacrificing our long standing human values in the interest of national and personal economic gain may be as repugnant to them as it is to us today.

Question #2
Will the concept of family lose its relevance for many of the children whom special education will be asked to serve?

The vast majority of program models utilized in both regular and special education over the past century have been predicated upon the existence of a traditional family support system. During the past three decades, a dramatic increase in the divorce rate has escalated the incidence of one-parent families in our society. The rise in births to single, teenaged mothers has become a serious social and educational problem. Each year thousands of children enter this world addicted to drugs and alcohol.

Not only are a disproportionate percentage of these children reflected within the ranks of special education, but, additionally, many of our students live in residential centers, group homes, or, even worse, are counted among this nation's homeless population. Every day I have a significant number of taxis pull up to my school and leave off children who live in a single motel room with their mother and siblings. Some of them travel as much as one hundred miles each day in order to obtain their schooling. My school, by the way, is located in a county whose per capita income is in the top one percent in the nation.

While we all wish that the human conditions were different (if only all children could be raised in a nurturing environment like we were), it just isn't so, and demographic forecasters do not see a big change coming. With this in mind, it behooves us as special educators to design affective learning opportunities that will provide, for these children, those things we were able to draw upon our family for. Counseling, child care, nutrition, health care providers, and alternative living arrangements must be developed in such a manner to both provide nurturing and promote self sufficiency. Special educators will need to work together with child advocates in the helping professions to creatively design solutions. They must also convince those who control public resources that there is significant merit in redesigning the support system for many children who would otherwise be denied their right to childhood.

Question #3
Can we improve our ability to infuse energy and enthusiasm into those special educators whose supply of both is constantly being drained by the children they serve?

During the 1980s, the concepts of stress and teacher burnout became popular items of discussion in educational circles. Wellness programs, professional circles, and staff development initiatives were designed to combat the potential impact of job stress common to those whose work place is the classroom.

Within special education, those who are most vulnerable to stress or burnout are usually teachers of children with severe mental retardation or emotional problems. Students who manifest serious behavior problems tend to place ongoing demands on their teacher, who frequently feels the impact of the students' non-stop attempts to have their emotional needs met. The teacher of individuals with severe mental retardation labors in an environment often devoid of verbal interaction. Due to the intensity of his or her students' limitations, the teacher often finds it difficult to assess the successes and growth that the children may be making. As a result, it is incumbent upon operators of special education programs to design and provide activities which effectively combat stress and burnout.

Involvement in professional organizations with others who work with similar students can be very helpful. This often leads to the opportunity to attend conferences and workshops which are instrumental in recharging teachers' batteries. Networking with other special education programs results in opportunities to exchange and share ideas, materials, and methods providing teachers with a new perspective on their job's challenges. Staff development activities within the system need to provide teachers with an outlet to openly discuss their work, both its joys and frustrations. Their supervisor needs to be aware of the warning signs of stress and burnout and needs to provide supportive intervention and creative suggestions for dealing with these issues.

While larger organizations offer the opportunity for teachers to change positions within the system for respite and a change of scenery, those who labor in small school districts are denied this luxury. Multi-district teacher exchanges can be effectuated and should be considered if they would serve the interests of everyone involved. When working with our most complex and challenging populations of students, a healthy and confident teacher needs to look forward each day to entering the special education classroom and meeting with his or her students. Creative ways of insuring that this will be happening needs to be discovered in the years ahead.

Question #4

Have the spirit and intent of the due process features of federal and state legislation been appropriately recognized and utilized to benefit and advocate for exceptional children?

At the time of the development of PL 94-142 and the various companion laws at the state level, it was considered important to protect the rights of exceptional children by creating due process provisions within those statutes that would allow parents to challenge the placement of their child in special education programs. Appeal procedures were designed aimed at the resolution of conflicts that might arise between parents and school districts when children were moving between the regular and special education systems.

It was widely expected that parents would be resistant to having their children placed in special education classes. It was also anticipated that school districts who wished to provide services would also utilize this process to advocate for the best interests of children who they desired to serve. During the past fifteen years, the acceptance of special education by parents as a viable and effective solution to their children's learning problems has increased dramatically. At the same time, school districts have been resistive to utilizing these provisions due to the costliness of the process and the fact that if they lose, they must pay the parents' legal fees.

Again it was believed, circa 1975, that the due process provisions, when utilized, would result in the child ultimately receiving the most appropriate level of services and greatly enhance his or her chances for success in school. When both the parents and the school were advocating strongly for what they believed was best for the child, it seemed inevitable that the compromise or ultimate decision would offer the child significant benefits.

Unfortunately, this desire on the part of those who drafted the legislation may well have missed its goal. Pushy parents often prevail at the initial stages of identification of their child's disability and school districts back off quickly to avoid conflict. Frequently, the parents demand excessive amounts of costly related services such as speech and occupational therapy where the professionals who supply them are in short supply. Unnecessary use of time and energy with children who don't need such a level of support only exacerbates this critical shortage of staff.

At the other extreme, there are far too many parents who do not choose to become involved in the process at all and allow school districts to do whatever they feel is best for their child. While I would like to think that district personnel always advocate for and make enlightened decisions about exceptional children, parents refraining from participating in the process can be dangerous. The basic bottom line is, if the due process provisions were designed to benefit children through the process of conflict resolution, and if either side backs away from the conflict or fails to challenge the process, the best interests of the child may be compromised. That risk should not be acceptable to those who consider themselves child advocates.

In the years ahead, we need to study the structure of our due process system and explore methods for utilizing the procedure in such a manner that will greater facilitate the intentions of those who drafted the legislation. A system that is more cost effective, offers less risks for school districts, and increases parental participation needs to be designed, if the best interests of children are to be served. I am confident that such a process can be designed and will ultimately bring to fruition the desired outcome that we set out to be accomplish fifteen years ago.

Question #5

Can we discover economic incentives for the technology industry to allocate a greater share of their

resources for the purpose of exploring methods of assisting the disabled?

Throughout the last decade, educators have been bombarded with sophisticated sales and marketing approaches touting the potential impact of instructional technology on young learners. Almost every school building now has available for its students a computer room where inquisitive young minds can explore the wonders of technology. Creative advances in both hardware and instructional software have resulted in computer assisted instruction becoming a crucial component of the educational landscape. Each school year the horizons of this technological movement expand, and teachers rush to improve their level of expertise in order to stay ahead of their more creative students.

Special educators have been working diligently to discover ways of better taking advantage of what these innovative instructional systems have to offer exceptional children. For the more mildly disabled students, there are a variety of intriguing drill and practice activities that allow children the opportunity to improve their academic skills. The research on the efficacy of these materials is supportive and the market for their utilization within special education is growing rapidly.

The real exciting aspect of technological potential for our field, however, rests with what it can offer for those learners who are more severely impaired. Learners who are deaf, blind, physically disabled, severely speech impaired, and multiply disabled can gain access to a much broader base for expressing their knowledge than ever before. By utilizing individually designed technological support systems, large segments of these disabled populations have the potential to overcome many learning problems that had previously been insurmountable. Each year new examples of the impact of computers in assisting such students excites special educators who strive to discover the latest innovation which may be the key for one of their students.

A major restraining force to the development of appropriate technology for the severely disabled has been the low incidence level of these particular disabilities. Also, many of the instructional support systems must be designed for individual learners. Unable to develop these materials for a mass market of consumers, the business of their research and design has become so costly that it is far beyond the ability of school districts to afford. What can be done with technology will only come about when we come up with a method for financially supporting the design and marketing efforts of those who manufacture the technology.

Special educators who serve those with severe disabilities need to work with government, business, private foundations, and health agencies to design both funding alternatives and more general products that utilize technology. It would seem that our ever growing population of senior citizens will also benefit from the development of many of these support systems and therefore have a vested interest in this field. Tax incentives for companies which are willing to invest their resources in creating new technological advances for the disabled of all ages should also be a consideration. We must do all we can to reward the creative minds that will discover ways to assist the severely disabled to access the benefits of technology in the twenty-first century.

Question #6
Can we develop a higher level of congruence between status and dignity as they pertain to the helping professions?

The direction of young people entering college today indicates to us that fewer of them are seeking careers serving their fellow human beings. What I refer to as the "A.P.K. Syndrome" appears to be sweeping the nation as college freshman major in areas of study that will quickly provide them with financial security similar to that of Alex P. Keaton of the 1980s sitcom **Family Ties** fame. Business, engineering, law, computer science and accounting enrollments in post-secondary institutions give evidence to the younger generations' interest in more profit- oriented career patterns.

While much of the motivation for this significant shift can be written off to financial considerations, serious reflection would lead us to consider the research that demonstrates the frighteningly low level of status associated with teaching and related helping professions. While lay people are quick to point out how "rewarding" our work must be for us, they stubbornly refuse to find a way to demonstrably reward us. It is assumed by the majority of Americans that those of us who work as special educators either accrue intrinsic rewards from what we do, or maybe are patient enough to wait for our compensation in the next life. Unfortunately, those entering college today do not appear motivated to react against such flawed logic.

Always enormously proud of the dignity of our profession, I must lobby for those who are to follow in our footsteps to increase the status of the helping professions. Demographic studies dramatically point out that the need for special education teachers, social workers, psychologists, speech therapists, and health professionals will increase at an alarming rate during the current decade. History demonstrates that those societies that have fallen frequently did so as a result of failure to nurture and reward their human values. We must indefatigably recruit and encourage the finest young people who are graduating from our high schools each year for the helping professions. Greater realization of the dignity of such work will result in better remuneration and the ultimate respect these individuals deserve.

Question #7
Has one of the unanticipated consequences of PL 94-142 been that regular education became more homogeneous while special education became more heterogeneous?

Back in the 1960s, the percentage of children identified and placed in special education classes was usually within the three to six percent range. As much as possible, administrators attempted to group children in a manner that resulted in relatively manageable classes of students with a common level of academic deficiency. With a four year age range, my classes would reflect academic levels of the same range, but each school district would likely only have one such class. These special education teachers cheerfully made do and grew to appreciate the diversity reflected within the classroom.

In the 1970s, while working in rural school districts, I observed that while the percentage of children placed within special education remained small, the regular education program was remarkably diverse in the population it served. Some districts grouped students in pre-first, first, pre-second, and second grade configurations based on the varied learning rates they were attempting to accommodate. A regular education teacher would not find it unusual at many grade levels to have a three or more year reading and/or math range within his or her classroom.

Looking around the affluent suburban region where I'm currently employed, I find nearly twelve percent of the K-12 population in need of special education services. Children who are mildly disabled constitute much of those in need of such support but the range of programs include such categories as: severely multiply handicapped, traumatic brain injured, seriously emotionally disturbed, communication disordered, and gifted/handicapped. Children whose level of intelligence cannot be accurately measured are served by our BOCES, as are students with IQs above 135 who also manifest emotional problems or learning disabilities.

We offer home instruction to new born infants and advanced placement courses for high school seniors who are gifted/handicapped. The diversity of what is available is mind boggling when compared to what was available twenty-five years ago.

Meanwhile, in the regular education classrooms within our region few, if any, teachers find themselves dealing with students who are below grade level academically. The popularity of special education as a viable alternative for children with learning problems has made life for the regular education teacher much less complex. Working each day with a room full of students who have proven their ability to meet the academic demands of the curriculum is most enjoyable.

Recognizing that this was not the intent of the federal and state legislation, we are now attempting some mid-course corrections. Pull-out programs are being redesigned to prevent the fragmentation that has frequently been an undesirable side effect. Consulting teacher models bring special educators into the regular education classroom to assist both students and teachers in accomplishing their goals. Staff development initiatives have been designed to help regular education teachers adjust their teaching styles to the learning styles of their students.

As we cautiously enter the 1990s, regular and special educators are beginning to work together to achieve consensus on their mutual responsibilities relative to students who are mildly handicapped and at-risk students. Hopefully, the results of these efforts will be a better and less restrictive balance of obligations within the total system of public education.

Question #8

Has the emphasis on compliance with federal and state laws and regulations resulted in the diminution of creativity and quality in the services being provided to exceptional children?

Throughout the years prior to the passage of monumental federal and state legislation impacting upon the field of special education, programs for exceptional children were recognized for their creative and imaginative instructional strategies. Due to the nature of the children we were attempting to serve, the special education teacher was challenged with the need to devise methods of infusing knowledge that were at best considered non-traditional. Driven by a desire to provide our students with instructional success experiences, there were little or no limitations on what kind of instructional designs we might incorporate into our educational programs.

With the onset of PL 94-142 and the various pieces of state legislation that closely followed, a gradual snuffing out of the flame of creativity that had for so long been the symbol of special education took place. Over-prescriptive regulations spelled out to program providers

178

what was or was not allowed. In a well-meaning attempt to bring every school district in our nation up to a minimum standard, we may have lost sight of the need to inspire everyone to continue moving forward toward the highest standard.

Creating this layer of monitoring personnel to insure compatibility with regulatory standards, we run the risk of moving all programs toward the middle of the quality spectrum. Isn't it time for courageous program providers to step forward and ask for creative freedom to attempt new program designs that will once again relight the flame of creativity? The needs of our students grow more complex annually, and if we do not grow with them in the designing of our solutions, we will invariably lose ground. Fifteen years of compliance monitoring should be a large enough litmus test of school districts' willingness to serve exceptional children.

Question #9
Should special education reserve its right to say no?

Those who have taken the time to study the roots of special education appreciate the work that teachers of the deaf and the blind conducted in the early years. Their search for instructional solutions makes for interesting reading and is most inspirational.

Itard's work with the "wild boy" began our search for the answers to questions relative to the educable nature of intelligence. With a much higher level of incidence, those with mental retardation became a heavy focus of special education in its formative years. Well into the middle part of the twentieth century, the major emphasis in training special educators dealt with the nature and needs of children with mental retardation.

Suddenly, during the 1960s, awareness of the instructional needs of children labeled "learning disabled" became in vogue. In addition, special educators were being asked to provide instruction for a growing number of students classified as having emotional disturbance or behavioral disorders. The needs of these two groups of students dramatically overwhelmed the attention of our profession and quickly became the vast majority of students being served under the new legislation.

Always willing to advocate for and serve children in need, special educators eagerly agreed to relieve the regular education system of the responsibility for adjusting to meet the challenges presented by these large numbers of students. Child-find quotas were quickly attained

179

as service providers opened resource rooms or center-based facilities to accommodate the onrushing hoard of students who felt reprieved from their failure experiences within the mainstream of public education.

While few challenged the course special education was taking, the issue of professional and moral responsibility for what was happening successfully avoided meaningful scrutiny. Special educators demonstrated their ability and parents grew to accept this parallel system as the best available answer to their child's problems.

Most recently, special educators have been given the challenge to respond to the instructional needs of infants and toddlers with disabilities. Seriously complicating matters is the fact that many of these children are addicted to drugs or alcohol. Others suffer from AIDS. Little or nothing appears to be known about the educational implications of their medical condition, nor does anyone suggest how special educators should proceed to develop meaningful service delivery systems for them.

Given our past history and future demands, special educators may need to focus upon the development of a clear mission statement that will establish parameters of responsibility for students across the ever-widening expanse of public education. While we have traditionally never said no when called upon to provide services for children with unique needs, we may wish to reserve the right to so decide. As our increasingly complicated society produces children with complex physical, mental, and emotional anomalies, special educators need to work with the regular education system and the medical profession to determine roles and relationships that will best serve the children of the next century. Proud of the accomplishments of our field, we should freely express our concerns when unrealistic or unfair expectations threaten the integrity of special education by attempting to stretch our skills and resources beyond realistic boundaries. In so doing, we should never lose sight of our objective of moving all children toward regular education and the benefits inherent within that system.

Question #10

Will the rapidly increasing emphasis on Vocational Rehabilitation for adults with disabling conditions call into question the efficacy of Special Education?

Those who advocate for the needs of adults with disabling conditions at the state and national levels have been quick to point out that the unemployment rate amongst the disabled is dramatically higher than that among adults who are non-disabled. Various reports call for the consideration of dramatic alternatives to traditional vocational training and placement of the disabled in our nation's work force. As the accumulation of discouraging statistics and cries for change increase, it is important that we carefully analyze what the data is telling us before we attempt to alter what appears to be a failing system.

In that PL 94-142 is more than fifteen years old, some pundits are quick to suggest that the high unemployment rate among adults with disabilities speaks unfavorably of the impact special education programs have had on those who have been so prepared for the world of work. To make such an accusation, however, denies the fact that the data on who are the unemployed with disabilities is seriously flawed, and that systemic barriers may have been responsible for much of this apparent failure.

Many of the unemployed adults with disabilities are individuals who spent most of their childhood and much of their adult life in institutional settings. Never recipients of special education, they are now located in community settings where local service agencies are just beginning to address their vocational training needs.

The large numbers of unemployed adults with disabilities who are listed as having physical disabilities is dramatically inconsistent with the data for the school-aged population with disabilities. This would lead one to believe that the onset of these physical problems took place during their adulthood, and they, too, were most likely not enrolled in special education.

This is not to deny that there were large numbers of secondary-level vocational education programs which were reluctant to develop training opportunities for students with disabilities. While in many regions of the nation such programs were slow in their creation, the efforts today at rectifying this condition are very encouraging.

One must surely agree with the need to train better and aggressively find employment for workers with disabilities. After a childhood where the funding for their education is sufficient, fiscal support for vocational rehabilitation is woefully lacking. We must do everything within our power to ensure that the successes of special education for children be replicated in the world of work for these individuals during their adulthood.

Question #11
Has the field of special education grown so much, so fast and become so bureaucratized that we have become adult-oriented rather than child-centered?

It seems like such a relatively short time ago that school districts only provided special education services for three percent of their total district enrollment. Today, it is more like twelve percent with many others being categorized as "at-risk" and in need of similar support.

During the 1960s, a special education staff meeting in a large suburban school district would bring together six to eight people. That same district today, with approximately the same student base, employs over fifty individuals to provide services for pupils with disabilities.

Expenditure levels in support of special education have grown just as dramatically. Recent estimates in **U.S. News and World Report** point out that expenditures for special education have grown from one billion dollars to thirty billion dollars since the passage of PL 94-142. We certainly cannot accuse federal and state legislators of not attempting to provide the necessary funding for special education.

In an attempt to manage this significant growth in an orderly fashion, the federal and state governments have developed a layer of bureaucracy whose purpose it is to insure compliance and conformity to law and regulations. The creation of the monitoring system has resulted in the necessity for many professionals to learn how to interrelate with each other over issues dealing with special education. Reports, complaints, hearings, appeals, reviews, and technical assistance have become avenues for local, state and federal employees to interface in the best interest of exceptional children.

In 1963, it cost my school district less then ten thousand dollars to operate my class of eight students. In 1970, I started my school for children with severe emotional disturbances with an allocation of two thousand dollars per student. By 1980, my cost in a rural poor intermediate unit was less than five thousand dollars per child. Now my average tuition rate in a large wealthy suburban BOCES will approach twenty-five thousand dollars. That budget is predicated on a student enrollment of six hundred exceptional children whose needs require me to employ over three hundred full- or part-time staff.

Class sizes within special education are a half or a third the size they were twenty-five years ago. The number of adults involved in serving our unique populations of students has increased dramatically. Related service providers have become critical components of the program as they provide speech, physical, and occupational therapy. Counselors, social workers, and psychologists assist us in relating more effectively to the students and their families. Computerized IEP's quickly determine appropriate goals and objectives for staff to focus upon each school year.

In 1963, I spent one hundred percent of my time each day focused upon meeting the needs of my eight students. From 1970 through 1972, eighty-five percent of my professional time at Hillside was dedicated to problem solving with and for the students in my school. In 1980, the challenges of operating a program for nearly four hundred children allowed me to spend close to seventy percent of my time dealing with child centered issues. Today, only fifteen percent of my work day deals with the unique needs of our children while the remaining eighty-five percent is spent responding to the concerns and issues of the various sectors of the public with whom we now relate.

I can't help but worry that this rate of growth within our field has somehow resulted in an undesired consequence. We must constantly fight to insure that our focus will always be the children for whom this multifaceted service system was developed. The importance of each adult within the system should be measured by the quality of service he or she can deliver to those for whom the system was developed. In so doing, they ultimately earn and deserve the label of advocate.

Question #12
How important is it to the future course of special education to reach final consensus on the issue of the Least Restrictive Environment?

Long before those who were responsible for drafting the federal and state statutes which currently drive special education programming had developed the concept of LRE, special educators had engaged in heated and emotional debate over the issue of instructional settings for programs serving exceptional children. Unaware of what sophisticated terminology might evolve relative to this concern, parents and advocates joined with special education professionals to discuss the relative merits of a variety of educational facilities and program designs.

Had those who initiated this cross section of programs realized the long term cultural, fiscal, and instructional impact of their decisions, they might well have been more hesitant to take on that responsibility. In fairness, however, they were working with a particular set of precon-ceived notions that proved to be extremely vulnerable to a significant switch in educational philosophy relative to services for children with disabilities. Their selection of appropriate venues for conducting educational programs for exceptional children were limited by such factors as the following:

- extremely poor locations for existing classes in school basements or local church halls.
- lack of social acceptance for the schools responsibility to educate children with mental or emotional disabilities.
- serious funding limitations which frequently colored their

decisions.

- lack of awareness that with the discovery of the concept of learning disabilities, the number of students entering special education would dramatically expand.

For most communities throughout the nation, a decision was originally made to either locate special education classes in their local school buildings or to construct large centers in which exceptional learners could receive appropriate instruction. The results of that decision have had a profound impact on how the residents of those communities perceive exceptional children and to what degree the new philosophical concepts contained in the legislation have been translated into meaningful programs.

Once special education centers are built, it is difficult to fully close them down -especially, if a retired superintendent or school board president has his or her name on the side of the building. In some areas of the country where the financial resources were not available to construct such centers, children with disabilities attended school with their non-disabled peers for three generations. Implementing the spirit and intent of the concept of the LRE has far-differing implications in these two settings which, incidentally, may only be a few miles apart geographically.

As the decade of the '80s wound to a conclusion, the arguments surrounding the fulfillment of the programmatic intentions of LRE grew significantly in intensity. With the development of the Regular Education Initiative (REI), it was hoped that those students with mild disabilities could receive appropriate services within the regular education classroom given the support of a consulting teacher. Numerous programs originally housed in separate centers for children with disabilities have relocated in local school buildings where mainstream instructional opportunities may be facilitated. In many areas, children whose level of mental retardation may have previously precluded their acceptance in local schools are now being served most effectively side by side with their non-disabled neighbors.

While this progress is long overdue in many regions of the nation, it is nonetheless a positive sign that the quality of life for exceptional children is improving in its direction toward achieving normalcy. Dissatisfied with this degree of progress, there are a growing number of parents and professionals who uncompromisingly advocate for the total inclusion of children with severe disabilities within the regular education system. They strongly feel that the social benefits of interacting with normal peers outweighs the academic value of a traditional special education program. Their emphasis on social change and the need to dismantle the system of special education as it has evolved in our country is centered around the interpretation of the intent of the LRE language in the law.

Arriving at an acceptable consensus on the true meaning of LRE is not something I would expect to witness in my lifetime. But the debate should go on if for no other reason than it fosters creativity in programmatic designs within both special and regular education. Progress toward normalization and movement of children back into regular education at a greater rate than they are referred to special education will always be a driving force in how we provide services. Extreme points of view that hold the potential for underserving exceptional children should be countered by rational arguments that point out the efficacy of quality programs existent within the service delivery system.

Having had the opportunity to provide services at each programmatic point along the traditional special education continuum of services, I understand both the strengths and limitations of each. The future decisions as to just which types of programs should be provided for exceptional children in the twenty-first century should best be determined by the academic progress and social gains of the children so served and far less by the rhetoric of those adults whose need it is to promulgate philosophical positions.

Question #13

In a time of limited fiscal and human resources, can we continue to provide extensive related services without supportive evidence of their effectiveness?

Growing concurrently with special education programming during the past twenty years has been the level of related services being provided to children with disabilities. Such services are an integral part of both the federal and state statutes and are necessary ingredients of a total individualized education plan (IEP). The inclusion of these services in the IEP require that school boards search for service providers and see that these mandates are appropriately met.

Speech, physical, and occupational therapy are frequently prescribed for exceptional children who manifest a variety of disabilities. Related counseling service is commonly recommended for children whose level of emotional disturbance warrants it. Provided by social workers or psychologists, counseling sessions emphasize the development of the requisite social skills necessary for the child to be successful in school and at home.

With the increased role of these related services within the field of special education, teams and committees who are charged with the development of IEP's must regularly wrestle with the questions of whether or not to prescribe these services and, if so, how frequently. Most of these services evolved out of the medical model and educators are usually reluctant to challenge the need for them. The jargon utilized by the professionals who provide these services frequently impresses, or more often, confuses those who are mandated to pass judgment on these issues.

Adding to the complexity involved in the process is the fact that the person who usually recommends to the team or committee that a particular child needs such a service is the only professional in the district who is qualified to provide that service. Skeptical administrators and school board members commonly raise this issue as they attempt to halt what they perceive as the runaway growth of special educational services. Convincing them that the professional behavior of the districts' staff is child-centered as opposed to self-serving is a challenge for many special education administrators.

Today there are some serious storm clouds on the horizon related to the provision of these services. A severe shortage of speech therapists, psychologists, and physical and occupational therapists has made service provision a luxury in many areas of the country. Under-graduate training programs for these professionals are inadequate for the current demand let alone the expected caseload for the years ahead.

Resistance to pull-out program models which has resulted in students missing important components in their educational program in order to receive related services is steadily growing in intensity. Scheduling a caseload in a cost-effective and educationally productive manner has become extremely difficult.

Complicating matters even worse is the fact that our ability to measure the effectiveness of many of the related services, in a manner that can be convincing to decision makers, is seriously limited. Counselors are able to explain why they feel particular students may be progressing or regressing, but most of their evidence is extremely subjective and therefore, difficult to quantify. Speech therapists who work with children with mental retardation experience difficulty in determining what role the mental retardation plays in language development and what level of progress we should expect to see each school year. Universities and clinics have not been eagerly addressing the need to develop measurement scales to assist us in this process despite the fact that the need for such measurement grows each year.

Some professionals are beginning to question the value of providing five sessions a week of speech therapy for children with severe mental retardation whose prognosis for ever developing meaningful language is remote at best. While the field of special education was built upon hope and the belief in human potential, the shortage of human resources in the area of related services may be forcing program providers to consider triage models to determine who should be the first recipients of service. As distasteful as this may be, unless standards of measurement used to detect progress in speech, counseling, etc., can give us clearer guidelines, or unless the supply of service providers dramatically changes, we may soon be faced with intense professional debate over rights to service. Such a reality would be a sad day in the history of special education in America.

Question #14
Will special education be able to successfully transfer some of its instructional practices into the regular education system?

Critics of the rapid growth in special education services are quick to point out what they feel is the over-identification of children with mild disabilities who comprise such a high proportion of those being served under state and federal mandates. Research demonstrates that children with learning problems in one community who remain within regular education perform better than children with similar needs in another community who are classified as learning disabled and who are served by special education programs. While this evidence is professionally disconcerting, little has been done to deter the growth rate of special education services for the mildly impaired.

However, educators recently have become increasingly disenchanted with the concept of pull-out programs for children with academic deficiencies. The evidence demonstrates that when such students leave the regular education classroom, in order to be provided with remediation for learning problems, they miss out on the instructional activities that are going on in class and thus fall farther behind.

Additionally, being identified as in need of service via traditional special education service models continues to carry a degree of stigma within the school that tends to be a disservice to mildly disabled learners. Rarely, if ever, does leaving the classroom for extra help in a resource room enhance a child's social status with either classmates or instructional staff.

As the special education delivery system has grown, the regular education program has incrementally become more homogeneous. An unwelcome consequence of this phenomenon has been the decreased level of ownership of responsibility for solving complex learning problems of children who are functioning below grade level. The ready availability of specialists and eager special educators has only complicated the problem. The increased awareness and identification of children who are now being referred to as "at-risk" may well intensify this trend.

Toward the latter part of the 1980s, the federal Office of Education began talking about and promoting the concept of the Regular Education Initiative (REI). In concept, the REI suggested that the regular education system become more proactive in attempting to meet the instructional needs of children with learning problems within the regular education classroom. Well meaning as this effort was, it was still a concept created by special educators who were attempting to draw regular education into the effort to serve children with mild disabilities within the mainstream. To imply that the initiative was, in fact, that of regular educators, may well have been a misnomer.

A recent trend, however, appears to offer significant potential for successfully providing special education services to children who are mildly impaired within the regular education system. Known as the **consulting teacher model**, this concept brings the special education teacher into the regular education classroom where she works in concert with the regular education teacher to provide meaningful instruction for identified students. In those schools where this practice has caught on, the results have been positive. It requires a unique set of skills on the part of the special educator and a high degree of openness and commitment on the part of the regular education teacher.

Question #15

Will the sociological and demographic changes facing our nation's schools in the years just ahead overwhelm special education and, by so doing, negatively impact upon its potential for serving exceptional children?

While the progress we have made in the field of special education during the preceding three decades has been significant, the challenges that today are emerging upon the horizon suggest that the future course of our profession could be most exciting. While the solution of previous problems has been a process that seemed well within our grasp, there are indications that orderly change in the years just ahead will be difficult to facilitate. Demographic studies strongly indicate that sociological factors will dramatically impact on our schools and the manner in which we provide educational services. How these factors influence special education will be directly related to how effectively we prepare ourselves to cope with them.

A recent study, that shocked those who read it, concluded that one in four children under the age of six in this nation is living below the poverty level. It has long been accepted that there is a strong correlation between poverty and poor school performance so we can well imagine how children with disabilities who live in poverty may have extensive barriers to overcome.

Futurists also predict that by the year 2000, one of three school children in our nation will be from a minority culture. Many of our urban centers experience this phenomenon now and find that many minority groups are over-represented within their special education program. It is not unlikely that the special education teacher of the future will be faced with a class of students whose divergent cultural backgrounds will impact upon instructional strategies within the classroom. As complicated as attempting to overcome students' disabilities conditions may be, this multi-cultural overlay will certainly extend the level of uniqueness within the special education profession.

At present, we are becoming more aware of the needs of three groups of students whose involvement in special education has not traditionally been a consideration. Children born of drug- or alcohol- addicted mothers and who manifest serious developmental problems are beginning to enter the schools, and special educators are being called upon to respond to their needs. Youngsters who manifest attention-deficit disorders are drawing greater interest from the medical community who, in turn, are asking schools to provide special educational programming for them. Parents of these children are aware of the success of special education programs for learning disabled and behaviorally disordered students and are demanding that their child's uniqueness be recognized and accommodated for. The third group wishing to be included under special education's umbrella of services is that of the children who have suffered some form of traumatic brain injury. Primarily victims of serious accidents, these students require a combination of rehabilitative therapies and careful instructional programming geared toward restoring their previous level of cognitive functioning. It is a complex challenge for those special education programs which see fit to adapt to serving them, and the growth they are able to bring about is most inspiring.

As special educators are and will be asked to extend themselves to serve more unique populations, administrators are concerned about the impact this will have upon the enrollment cap that the federal government has placed upon states under PL 94-142. Presently, no state is permitted to claim, for federal funding purposes, more than twelve percent of its total K-12 student population. If the societal and demographic predictions are accurate, will both the state and federal funding sources recognize the need for fiscal support for meeting these significantly more unique and costly services?

In order to prepare ourselves for the demands that will be placed upon special education in the years ahead, we need to more aggressively recruit young people of high quality who may desire to serve exceptional children. All of the significant victories of the past will be of little value unless we can successfully pass on future responsibility to individuals whose tenacity and dedication will be commensurate with that of those who have preceded them as special educators. As a profession, we must and will be equal to the challenge of avoiding a dramatic swing of the pendulum that would lessen our national commitment to exceptional children. By providing high-quality, cost-effective services through the indefatigable efforts of dedicated special educators, we will be successful ultimately in meeting the ever-expanding needs of our nation's most challenging students.

And so, the legacy of the past three decades will have its quality determined by our ability to effectively answer many of the questions we have just explored. The success of our endeavors to reach acceptable solutions may well be dictated by the processes we utilize. Needing to expand the level of ownership by all those who are stakeholders in the future well-being of special education services, we should always maintain the child-centered focus that has so epitomized our profession.

Human values, consistent with the historical evolution of American society, must be the driving force insuring the equality of educational opportunity for those whom we recognize as exceptional. The brightest, most highly creative and energetic professionals will need to engage in the dialogue that searches for the answers to the questions of the next decade. Only by capturing our most valuable human resources with whatever financial resources are obtainable, will special education be able to continue its laudatory record of accomplishment with exceptional children.

It is my most sincere hope that you have enjoyed our journey through time which found us in the company of our nation's most unique children. As your tour guide, I have been exceedingly mindful of the impact each child has had upon my personal and professional growth. This process has significantly reinforced the beliefs that created the need for us to take this trip together. Thanks for coming along, and I'm sure that you will continue to enjoy the beauty of human difference for many years to come.

≈ *About the Author* ≈

Mark Costello is currently the Director of Special Education at the Putnam/Northern Westchester BOCES in Yorktown Heights, New York.

Those who are interested in sharing their experiences about exceptional children with him can write to him at 122 Arthursburg Road, LaGrangeville, New York, 12540.